STONEHENGE
Making sense of a
prehistoric mystery

Archaeology for All
Council for British Archaeology

STONEHENGE
Making sense of a prehistoric mystery

Mike Parker Pearson *with*
Joshua Pollard, Colin Richards,
Julian Thomas and Kate Welham
Illustrations by:
Peter Dunn, Adam Stanford and Irene de Luis

Archaeology for All
Council for British Archaeology 2015

Archaeology for All
Council for British Archaeology 2015
Published in 2015 by the Council for British Archaeology
Beatrice de Cardi House, 66 Bootham, York YO30 7BZ

British Library Cataloguing-in-Publication Data
A catalogue record for this book is available from the British Library
ISBN 978-1-909990-02-9

DOI: 10.11141/AfA2

Typeset by Carnegie Book Production
Printed and bound by The Lavenham Press Ltd

Cover images
Front: View south-west across the Stonehenge landscape © Adam Stanford
Back: Reconstruction painting of Bluestonehenge © Peter Dunn

Contents

List of figures

All photographs © Adam Stanford unless otherwise indicated

List of figures

Foreword

Ancient sites are like people: you can love the way they look, but you will never understand them unless you know more about their background. Archaeologists refer to this background as context. Put simply, context is everything: the landscape setting, the date, and the culture of the people at the time. As you will discover in this book, the context of Stonehenge is immensely complex and almost unimaginably rich. We now know that Europe's best-known prehistoric monument is far, far more ancient than anyone had suspected until very recently.

Like an extraordinary-looking person, Stonehenge has always attracted myths, legends and stories. I am sure this is because it is so striking, but yet so subtle. It doesn't dominate a hilltop, like the cathedrals at Durham or Lincoln, and by prehistoric standards it isn't particularly large: the nearby sites of Silbury Hill and Avebury, for example, are physically vast. But still it is unique: the dressed stones, the massive uprights and lintels are instantly recognisable. Draw two thick vertical lines and cap them with another, then show it to almost anyone anywhere in the world and they will say 'Stonehenge'.

In the past, attempts to explain Stonehenge and to understand why it was built have focused on the Stones themselves. But as Professor Mike Parker Pearson and his team have so triumphantly demonstrated, the Stones are by no means the whole story. The truth lies in the landscape surrounding them. In fact we will never understand what made our ancestors create this still magically haunting structure until we can place it in context. And that is what Mike and his team have done with such rigorous conviction. Thanks to them, we can now begin to answer the double question: 'Who built Stonehenge – and why?'

Francis Pryor
former CBA President

Understanding
the monument

To Stonehenge ... Came thither and find them as prodigious as
any tales I've ever heard of them and worth the journey to see.
God knows what their use was.

Samuel Pepys

Stonehenge is the last great stone circle of prehistoric
Britain. It was built and rebuilt over almost a thousand
years at the end of an era of megalith-building across
western Europe. The earliest megaliths of western Europe are
the standing stones and stone tombs of Brittany and Portugal,
constructed *c* 4700 BC when Neolithic farming communities came
into contact with indigenous hunter-gatherers along the coastal
zones of Atlantic Europe. By 3500 BC, megalithic monuments for
the dead were being built from Scandinavia to Britain and Ireland
to southern Spain; by 2500 BC the megalith-building boom was
over everywhere except in Britain and Ireland. Stonehenge is
among the very last of Europe's great megalithic monuments.

Mesolithic beginnings

Before the arrival of agriculture, the people of Britain and western
Europe lived by hunting and gathering. This period lasted in
Britain from the end of the Ice Age until 4000 BC and is known as
the Mesolithic, or Middle Stone Age. Stone tools included flaked
flint axe-heads mounted in wooden handles, and tiny pieces of
flint blades known as microliths that were hafted onto bone,

Figure 1.1 *(facing
page) Excavating
within Stonehenge
in 2008. From L-R:
Chris Casswell, Mike
Pitts, Jacqueline
McKinley (in pit),
Christie Willis and
Julian Richards*

Figure 1.2
Excavations in progress at Star Carr in 2013. The shore of the lake can be seen at top left, with waterlogged wood preserved in the shallow waters of the lake edge (© POSTGLACIAL)

wood or antler to make arrows, knives and saws. The best-known Mesolithic occupation site in Britain is Star Carr in Yorkshire, beside what was once a prehistoric lake in the Vale of Pickering. People gathered at Star Carr at certain times of the year during the Early Mesolithic period and may even have lived there for long periods of time, bringing the carcasses of wild animals that they had hunted around the lake edge.

Sites such as Star Carr are rare so it is very exciting that archaeologists recently found what may be a similar site beside a long-vanished lake or stream close to Stonehenge. About a mile (1.5km) to the east of Stonehenge, where the River Avon twists and turns in a series of meanders through the modern town of Amesbury, lies the site of Blick Mead. While excavations have been limited so far, tens of thousands of Mesolithic stone tools have been found here, along with wild animal bones that date from shortly after the time of Star Carr, *c* 7500 BC, through to *c* 4300 BC.

Understanding the monument

Blick Mead is likely to have been a seasonal gathering place or a home base, where groups of hunters lived on the edge of a lake and shared their prey – the wild pigs, deer and wild cattle attracted to the lake edge. Whereas Star Carr's lake had turned to swamp by *c* 6500 BC, the waterside at Blick Mead continued to attract people and animals for a further 2000 years, making it the longest-lived place for Mesolithic gatherings in Britain.

Four huge pits dating to the Early Mesolithic period were found at Stonehenge itself, under the former visitor centre and its car park. Three of these had once held very large posts. Hunter-gatherers are not generally known for building spectacular monuments, so these are something of a mystery. The postholes were uncovered just 400m north-west of Stonehenge in 1967, during the construction of the car park. The three pits were aligned east–west and each once held a large post of pine up to a metre in diameter. Carbonised wood from the scorched sides of two of the posts was later radiocarbon-dated and found to date to *c* 8000 BC, though it seems that not all three posts were standing at the same time.

The Stonehenge Mesolithic posts are pretty well unique. In southern Scandinavia there are a couple of examples of pits that once held monumental posts but otherwise nothing that matches the Stonehenge array. Despite 50 years of large-scale excavations across western Europe, the Stonehenge posts are unrivalled as Mesolithic monuments. They date to the earliest stages of Blick

Figure 1.3 *Recent finds from the excavations at Blick Mead (© Barry Bishop)*

Figure 1.4 *3D reconstruction of how the Mesolithic pine posts discovered below the car park at the old Stonehenge Visitor Centre might have looked (© Henry Rothwell)*

Mead so it is likely that people gathering there were responsible for erecting them.

The earliest Neolithic farmers of western Europe, by contrast, built monuments in profusion. Where stone was freely available, these took the form of megaliths; elsewhere they were composite earthen and wooden structures, such as long barrows. The vast majority of monuments contained the remains of the dead. These were not just Neolithic tombs but monuments for the ancestors, built to mark territorial claims. They were also community-building exercises by dispersed groups of farmers learning how to mobilise sufficient labour to plough and harvest successfully. In such kin-based societies, people traced their connections back in time to a shared ancestor or predecessor, in the way that cousins share the same grandparents and second cousins the same great-grandparents.

The initial process of domestication in the Near East *c* 9500 BC involved not just animals and crops but also social and cultural transformations in the way that people lived. Large, densely populated settlements were formed of substantial houses in which the dead were often buried under the floors. This symbolic and physical elaboration of the house was one way in which people 'domesticated' society along with the crops and animals. As agriculture spread into Europe *c* 5500 BC so the farmers' houses became large and monumental. By the time that farming reached the dispersed populations of western Europe, the tomb of the dead rather than the house of the living had become the monumental dimension of daily life. Houses along the western fringes of Europe were small, wooden and temporary; the tombs were large, megalithic and permanent. These 'houses of the dead' magnified certain features of domestic architecture taken from the two styles of house used by different groups of early farmers: round houses and rectangular houses.

The arrival of farming – the Early Neolithic

Just how farming arrived in Britain is not fully understood. Domestic sheep, cattle and pigs and domesticated cereals of wheat and barley were certainly brought across the English Channel in boats, but archaeologists do not know whether Continental farmers arrived en masse, whether indigenous hunter-gatherers themselves adopted agriculture, or whether there was a long prelude of cross-Channel interaction between both sides. Nor do we know how farming was adopted once it reached Britain. Some archaeologists argue for its arrival first in Kent, just 22 miles (35km) from the coast of France, but others propose its earliest arrival in Ireland and western Britain, prior to arrivals in the south and south-east of England. For some reason, it took 700 years before domesticated crops and animals crossed to Britain from the Continent, having been adopted along the European coast by 4700 BC. This suggests that the English Channel was a significant barrier, both cultural and physical.

Figure 1.5 *Kit's Coty House, near Aylesford, Kent, is a megalithic dolmen dating from the Early Neolithic. It is close to Coldrum, one of the first megaliths to be built in Britain*

The first megaliths to be built in Britain are likely to be the tombs of the Medway valley in Kent; one of these at Coldrum contained human bones dating to *c* 3900–3800 BC. Early Neolithic tombs of earth, chalk and timber were built in the Stonehenge area but none has been dated earlier than 3700 BC. However, we know that people were living in the valleys around Stonehenge, and gathering in large numbers there, by 3800–3700 BC because of a remarkable discovery on the high ridge between Stonehenge and Amesbury. This is a site called Coneybury, where Julian Richards excavated a large pit containing quantities of broken pots and animal bones. The bones included ten cattle and seven roe deer, along with other animals, and had been freshly butchered when thrown into the pit. Such

a meat feast could have fed a hundred people or more. Just why the remains of this feast were dumped in a specially dug pit is unexplained but it reveals that the Stonehenge locality was still a special place for gatherings hundreds of years after Blick Mead was abandoned, and many hundreds before Stonehenge itself was erected.

As well as building tombs, Britain's early farmers also constructed gathering places that we call 'causewayed enclosures' because their surrounding ditches have multiple causeways between them. It is likely that these causeways dividing the ditches into segments marked the different groups taking part in the gatherings, with each responsible for a particular segment of ditch and together forming the collective encircling enclosure.

Figure 1.6
Reconstruction drawing of Whitehawk Camp causewayed enclosure, near Brighton. The Camp, which dates from c 3600 BC, consists of four circuits of interrupted ditch and bank, the largest measuring c 300m x 200m and enclosing an area of c 6ha (© Ian Dennis)

Understanding the monument

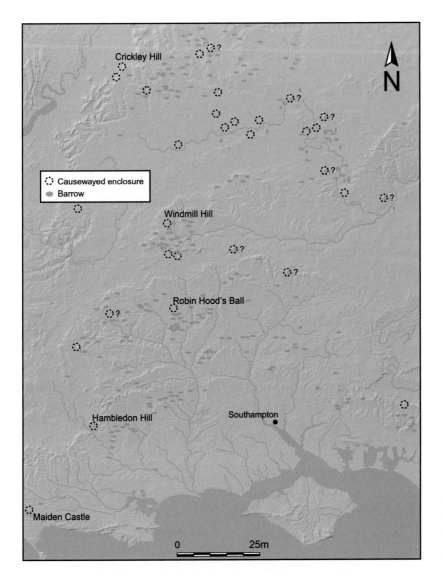

Crickley Hill

Windmill Hill

Robin Hood's Ball

Hambledon Hill

Southampton

Maiden Castle

○ Causewayed enclosure
● Barrow

N

0   25m

Figure 1.7 *Map of causewayed enclosures and long barrows in central southern England (© Irene de Luis)*

Most of these causewayed enclosures were built *c* 3650 BC but the one nearest Stonehenge, Robin Hood's Ball, some 4 miles (6.5km) to the north-west, was not constructed until a century or so later. The number of people who dug out the ditches and feasted on the animals whose bones were dumped in them need not have been more than 200 or so, but this still shows that the Stonehenge area was a place of gathering, whether sporadic or more regularly.

Monument types: long barrows, causewayed enclosures and cursus monuments

What people choose to monumentalise tells us much about their society. The Neolithic people of Britain and western Europe monumentalised places associated with their dead and their ancestors. Their houses were small, simple wooden buildings but their tombs and other places associated with the dead were huge and imposing structures. In Britain these monumental structures took the form of tombs (long barrows, long cairns, round barrows, dolmens, passage graves and chamber tombs), enclosures (causewayed enclosures, formative henges, classic henges), stone circles and cursus monuments.

Long barrows (c 3800–3600 BC for the main period of construction) are mounds of soil and chalk heaped high on top of fairly small wooden or stone structures or 'chambers', most of which contained the collective remains of the dead. A single tomb might contain the remains of tens of individuals, sometimes as separate skeletons or in other cases heaps of disarticulated bones. Around 3500 BC there was a move to individual burial and some long mounds of this date, such as Winterbourne Stoke barrow near Stonehenge, were erected over just one individual. Most long barrows have parallel ditches from which the earth that forms the mound was extracted. Long barrows are thought to be monumentalised versions of rectangular houses.

Causewayed enclosures (c 3800–3400 BC) are among the earliest forms of enclosures seen in Europe (first constructed on the Continent c 5500 BC) and were created by digging lengths of ditches, with gaps or causeways being left in place between each section. This

Figure 1.8 *Belas Knap, situated on Cleeve Hill, Gloucestershire, is an excellent example of a Neolithic chambered long barrow. Some 54m in length and 18m wide, it contains four separate burial chambers. The imposing entrance façade at the north end was purely for show – access to the chambers was via side passages. The stone wall around it is of recent date*

Figure 1.9 *The interior of West Kennet long barrow, near Avebury, Wiltshire*

arrangement of multiple entrances means these sites were of little use for defence from attacks, so they must have had some other purpose. The ditch segments are thought to have been dug by different work-gangs, emphasising a co-operative effort by separate groups. At many causewayed enclosures, such as Robin Hood's Ball near Stonehenge, the ditches filled up with the debris from feasting. Human remains in various degrees of disarticulation were also deposited, along with stone axes, pottery and other artefacts that had sometimes originated far from the locality. Causewayed enclosures were gathering sites where alliances could be formed and disputes resolved. Around 3400 BC, two causewayed enclosures at Hambledon Hill and Crickley Hill were turned into defensive sites and definitely suffered attacks, possibly as part of a wider conflict that gripped south-west England at that time.

Cursus monuments (c 3600–3200 BC) are long, narrow, rectangular enclosures surrounded by a ditch and a bank. They appear to be monumental versions of the rectangular mortuary enclosures of timber or stone found under long barrows. Their earliest appearance is in eastern Scotland c 3700 BC, where their edges are marked by timber posts. Cursus monuments can be over 6 miles (9.5km) long but most are no longer than a mile or so. They are some of the largest of a series of earthen and timber monuments that includes long mortuary enclosures and an elongated type of barrow known as a bank barrow. As with long barrows, their architectural form is that of a monumentalised rectangular house.

Understanding the monument

The Middle Neolithic

Sometime around 3500 BC people gathered in the Stonehenge locality to dig the ditches for a pair of long, narrow enclosures, the largest of which is 1¾ miles (2.8km) long and up to 150m wide. The antiquary William Stukeley discovered this larger example in the 18th century and thought it might be a Roman chariot-racing track, so he named it 'the Cursus'. The name, however inappropriate, has stuck; it is definitely not Roman, and it had nothing to do with chariot-racing, but it is still known as the Greater Stonehenge Cursus, to distinguish it from the Lesser Cursus.

Figure 1.11 Map showing cursus monuments, major henges and stone circles in central southern England (© Irene de Luis)

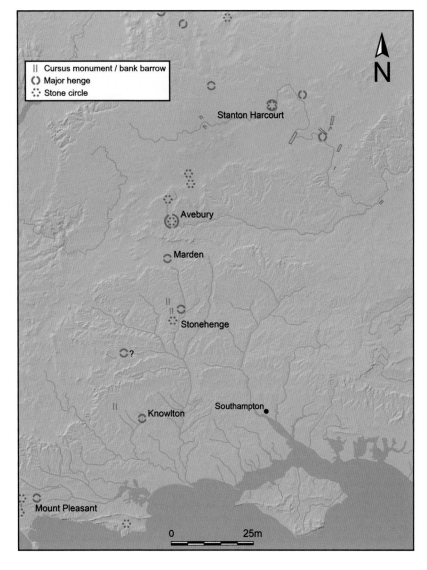

Figure 1.12 *The spectacular megalithic tomb of Newgrange, near the Bend in the Boyne, Ireland. Constructed c 3200 BC, the mound is 80m in diameter and covers an area of almost half a hectare. It is surrounded by 97 kerbstones*

Over 100 of these so-called 'cursus' monuments have been found across Britain. All would have required considerable communal effort. In the case of the Greater Cursus, it has been calculated that if the ditches were dug in one operation, it would have required up to 1000 people. The east end of the Greater Cursus terminates at a long barrow, so it is likely that the monument had some association with the dead; indeed it is thought that cursus monuments may be enlarged versions of long mortuary enclosures. The tomb at the east end of the Greater Cursus was built around the same time. It was initially dug into in the mid-19th century by John Thurnam who found no human remains under the mound, only an ox skull, but

Understanding the monument

excavations in 2008 recovered a human humerus dating to
c 3200 BC. The arm bone had been washed into the ditch and
there was no sign of the rest of the body in this badly disturbed
mound. It is possible that this long barrow was built for only
one person. Long barrows built during the period 3800–3500
BC tend to contain the collective remains of many people but
long barrows built after 3500 BC were often built for just one
or two people's remains. This trend towards single burial is
well documented across Britain at that time. Sometimes the
deceased was provided with lots of grave goods, implying that
the individual and their family were of high social status. Such
burials beneath large mounds are also known from the Thames
valley, Yorkshire and the Peak District.

The act of building a mound for a single person is also a clear
indication of the emergence of inequality, replacing the ethos of
Early Neolithic collective burial with a new, individualised notion
of social hierarchy. There is one such single burial from under
a large long barrow 1½ miles (2.5km) to the west of Stonehenge
at Winterbourne Stoke Crossroads, dated to c 3500 BC. The
man buried here was about 30 years old and had grown up in
western Britain, and while his only grave good was a 20cm-long
flint implement, the collective effort of building the long mound
is a measure of his (and his family's) social standing in the
community.

More dramatic tombs were being built in Ireland at this time.
The enormous megalithic tombs of Newgrange and Knowth,
situated at the Bend in the Boyne, were built c 3200 BC. They
embody several important elements that we see a few centuries
later at Stonehenge. Firstly, they were composed of stones of
different types brought from many different locations miles
away from the River Boyne. Secondly, Newgrange was built with
a special stone 'light box' that allowed the midwinter solstice
sun to shine along the tomb's entrance passage into the end
chamber. Thirdly, these tombs contained the cremated remains
of the dead, not their bodies, a fashion in mortuary practices
that would take hold across Britain between 3000 and 2400 BC.

The period between 3500 and 3000 BC was clearly a time when
certain of the dead were more important than others. Large tombs
were being built in Britain to commemorate particular individuals,
not groups of people. Earlier mortuary rituals, that focused on
groups of ancestral remains, were replaced by burials of individual
ancestors.

Stone circles and henges

Stonehenge is both a stone circle and a henge. Stone circles are found throughout Britain and Ireland, although they are absent in parts of lowland eastern Britain where there are no stone outcrops. Stone circles date from *c* 3200 BC to 1500 BC. The large stone circles mostly date to the 3rd millennium BC. In Orkney, the Stones of Stenness date to *c* 2900 BC and the much larger Ring of Brodgar probably to *c* 2500 BC, while Calanais [Callanish] in the Outer Hebrides was built *c* 2800 BC. Most of the stone circles built after 2000 BC are relatively small and have orthostats (standing stones) less than a metre high.

Henges are banked and ditched circular enclosures that are found only in Britain and Ireland, and not in Europe. Although the term derives from Stonehenge, it does *not* refer to standing stone or timber structures. Stonehenge is an early type known as a 'formative' henge; these have an outer ditch and an inner bank. Stonehenge has, in addition, a slight outer bank or counterscarp. Formative henges (*c* 3200–2800 BC) were generally places of burial and sometimes incorporated stone circles and other standing stone settings. Classic henges are enclosures where the bank has been placed outside the ditch. They date from *c* 2900 BC to 1800 BC. Classic henges appear to have been commemorative, built on a spot to mark a particular event or the place where a special structure once stood. For example, Britain's largest henge, Durrington Walls, situated 1¾ miles (2.8km) north-east of Stonehenge, was built on top of a large village that was probably where the builders of Stonehenge lived.

Circles of timber were also built at this time: good examples are the Northern and Southern Circles at Durrington Walls. Occasionally timber circles were enclosed within henges, as is the case with Woodhenge, situated next to Durrington Walls. Such timber circles might also be replaced by stone monuments, as is also thought to have happened at Woodhenge (although these standing stones were later removed).

Figure 1.13 *The Ring of Brodgar, Orkney, lies close to the recently excavated settlement at the Ness of Brodgar (see Fig 4.5)*

The Late Neolithic: Stonehenge stage 1, c 2900 BC

Around the same time as Newgrange and Knowth were built, a new style of circular monument appeared in Britain, possibly originating in Wales. This was a circular ditch with an internal bank and one or more entrances into the interior of the encircled area. One of these was recorded at Llandygai, near Bangor in north Wales, before it was destroyed by development in the 1960s. Another now lies partly under a new road layout at Flagstones in Dorchester, Dorset. Further examples are known from Dorchester-on-Thames in Oxfordshire and in the Colne valley in west London. These circular enclosures, or 'formative henges', are associated with the cremated remains of the dead. At some of them there is evidence that standing stones were originally set up inside them or just beyond their entrances. Stonehenge itself, built c 2900 BC, is the latest known example of these 'formative henges'.

This first stage of Stonehenge was a circular ditched enclosure with its main entrance to the north-east and a smaller one to the south. The enclosure also had a slight outer bank, known as a counterscarp. Just inside the circuit of the inner bank there was a circle of 56 pits which archaeologists call the Aubrey Holes, named after the 17th-century antiquary John Aubrey. Holes for stones in the north-east entrance show that there may have been a line of three standing stones running north-east out of the entrance, associated with rows of wooden posts running perpendicular to this line of stones.

There were other arrangements of posts inside the Stonehenge circle, forming a pathway from the south entrance to the centre and also a series of small rectangular enclosures, one of which appears to have had a large standing stone within it. No one knows what these wooden structures were for but some may have been aligned, albeit imprecisely, on the major southern moonrise towards the south-east. The closest comparisons to these structures are the mortuary enclosures found normally under long barrows. The wooden post rows in the north-east entrance also have an approximate lunar orientation, facing out of the entrance towards the rising moon's northerly limit. While some authors have reckoned that these entrance posts were used by astronomer-priests for calendrical purposes, astronomer-archaeologist Clive Ruggles has pointed out that the 2° imprecision in the alignment is an indication that its purpose was symbolic rather than operational.

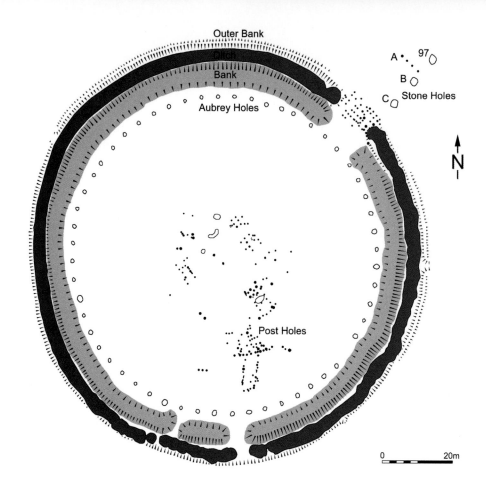

Figure 1.14
Stonehenge stage 1, c 2900 BC; the circular enclosure contains a single ring of bluestones in the Aubrey Holes and arrangements of timber posts in the interior
(© Irene de Luis)

Do these post rows and other aspects of Stonehenge's layout mean that Stonehenge was built as an astronomical observatory? New research suggests something rather different. From its beginning, Stonehenge was a cemetery. We know that it held the cremated remains of probably well over 100 people. The remains of 63 cremation burials have been excavated at Stonehenge, many from the Aubrey Holes and the ditch, and these are likely to be fewer than half of those originally buried here. This is the largest single burial ground known from this period anywhere in Britain.

There is evidence that some standing stones were put up at Stonehenge in this earliest stage, and although they have been removed, the holes in which they stood have survived. The large sizes of the three in a line beyond the north-east entrance indicate that these were most likely of the local sarsen stone. Sarsen is a type of sandstone or 'silcrete' formed 55 million years ago from conglomerated sand and is common today in parts of southern England, especially the Marlborough Downs 20 miles (32km) north of Stonehenge. Sarsens are also found in the Stonehenge

Understanding the monument

landscape, for example the Cuckoo Stone near Woodhenge, but seem to have been far less numerous here than further north. Sarsen is difficult to split even with steel tools; prehistoric stonemasons used heavy mauls and hammerstones to chip off large flakes and to pound the surface to the required shape. One sarsen stone that has not been shaped or dressed is the Heel Stone, which lies beyond the north-east entrance to Stonehenge. This lack of tooling may be evidence that it was set up in this position, or close to it, from the earliest stage of Stonehenge, long before the other stones were shaped. Famously, the sun rises just to the left of the Heel Stone on the midsummer solstice when viewed from the centre of Stonehenge.

The name of the Heel Stone carries no ancient meaning: the name of 'Heel' or 'Friar's Heel' was given in the 17th century, when local tradition told of the wizard Merlin being hit in the heel by the Devil throwing a large stone. The actual stone with a cavity

Figure 1.15
Stonehenge as it would have looked in stage 1 (© Peter Dunn)

Figure 1.16 *The Heel Stone, as it appeared before the road closure in 2013. Situated just outside the north-east entrance to Stonehenge, excavations have shown it may originally have been one of a pair*

resembling a footprint is recorded as lying within the west side of Stonehenge, but in 1771 the name of 'Heel Stone' was mistakenly attributed to this eroded outlier on the north-east of Stonehenge, and the name has stuck.

Excavations in the centre of Stonehenge have revealed several holes for long-vanished standing stones that are likely to have been of sarsen. One of them appears to have sat within the centre of one of the wooden structures. Only recently have archaeologists confirmed that there was a complete stone circle, 87m in diameter, within this first stage at Stonehenge. This was first suggested by William Hawley, who excavated most of the Aubrey Holes on the east side of Stonehenge *c* 1920 and noted that the bottoms and sides of many of these pits had crush-marks resulting from the pressure of a standing stone being inserted and later withdrawn.

Understanding the monument

He realised that these stones could only have been thin pillars, and could not have been the broad and chunky sarsens of which Stonehenge is primarily composed today. Hawley was referring to the stones known as 'bluestones', a variety of different types of stone, most of which have their origins in north Pembrokeshire in Wales, some 140 miles (225km) to the west of Stonehenge. The majority of the bluestones surviving at Stonehenge today are of spotted dolerite, a type of igneous rock found in the Preseli mountains of Pembrokeshire. Others are of rhyolite (sheet lava), argillaceous tuff, and sandstone. The surviving and undamaged bluestones at Stonehenge today stand to *c* 2m high, much smaller than the 4m-high sarsens.

Unfortunately Hawley's records were largely ignored by later archaeologists and he himself later doubted his initial conclusions so did not pursue his idea. Yet it is clear that the sizes and shapes of the Aubrey Holes are indistinguishable from those of holes into which bluestones were definitely later inserted at Stonehenge. As we will explore in Chapter 4, one of the Pembrokeshire quarries for the bluestones has revealed that these pillars were extracted *c* 3300 BC, in plenty of time to be erected at Stonehenge *c* 2900 BC.

A second, much smaller circle of bluestones was erected, probably at the same time (*c* 2900 BC), beside the River Avon at West Amesbury. This circle, some 20m in diameter, comprised approximately 25 stones and has come to be known as Bluestonehenge. The stones were pulled out *c* 2400 BC, leaving voids and impressions which show that they were thin pillars of the type that we recognise as bluestones, rather than the thicker and squatter sarsens.

Hawley's records are not good enough to know exactly where and how cremated remains were deposited within the Aubrey Holes (top, bottom, middle, sides and so on), but he did record that at least one burial was made after a stone pillar had been withdrawn. Much later, in 1950, Richard Atkinson recorded cremated bones in a deposit of chalk fill that we think was the packing to support a standing stone. This and other burials have recently been radiocarbon-dated, revealing that Stonehenge was a place of burial for over 500 years after it was first built. The cremated remains of men and women of all ages were buried at Stonehenge, although children were largely excluded. Very few objects were buried with the remains; one cremation deposit contained a stone mace-head (see Fig 3.14). Hawley observed that some of the cremation deposits formed small circles in their burial pits which suggests that the cremated remains were packed into leather bags before they were buried. Bone or antler pins found with some of the burials might have been used to secure the mouth of the bag. The number of people buried at Stonehenge declined after *c* 2700 BC and by the time the last cremated remains were buried *c* 2500 BC, Stonehenge had been completely rebuilt.

Stonehenge is the last of the 'formative henges' but this stage of its development coincides with the earliest of Britain's classic henges. Readers might be surprised to learn that Stonehenge is not a 'classic henge' when it is obvious that its name has given us the archaeological term 'henge'. Yet archaeologists use the term 'henge' to refer not to stone circles or ditched enclosures with internal banks but to enclosures in which the ditch is *inside* the bank. Classic henges are earthworks designed to focus

Figure 1.18 *The unusual Church Henge at Knowlton, Dorset, with the 12th-century Norman church constructed in the interior. There are two further henges close by, as well as numerous barrows*

inwards, as if something was being enclosed. The earliest dated example of a classic henge is in the islands of Orkney, off the north coast of Scotland, where the Stones of Stenness stone circle was enclosed by a bank and internal ditch dating to *c* 2900 BC. Today Orkney seems to be peripheral to the centre of Britain but it was a booming centre of megalith-building in the period 3400–2400 BC. Archaeologists see it as a centre of innovation and influence, an extraordinary place that developed novel fashions in architecture, both domestic and monumental. Classic henges such as the Stones of Stenness may have originated in Orkney and then spread to the rest of Britain, along with the square and rounded domestic architecture of the sort so well-preserved in stone at the settlement of Skara Brae.

Classic henges were certainly the first monumental architectural style to spread across the whole of Britain. Examples include the Thornborough henges in Yorkshire and the four great henge enclosures of the Wessex chalklands at Avebury, Marden, Mount Pleasant in Dorset, and Durrington Walls close to Stonehenge. Accompanying this Orkney-derived spread of architectural styles was a similarly Orcadian style of pottery, known as Grooved Ware. Its earliest appearance in Orkney was *c* 3200 BC, and we know that it was a quickly adopted ceramic fashion since it had reached the south coast of England by *c* 2800 BC; it then remained in vogue for another 500 years.

Solstices and major lunar standstills

The main astronomical events marked at Stonehenge are the extreme points of the rising and setting of the sun and moon. The sun reaches the most northerly points where it rises (in the north-east) and sets (in the north-west) on the longest day of the year on 21–22 June. This is the midsummer solstice when the sun's arc across the sky is longest. It follows its shortest arc, rising in the south-east and setting in the south-west, at the midwinter solstice on 21 December.

The movement of the moon is more complicated. It regularly reaches extreme points of rising and setting (known as minor lunar standstills) in the same way as the sun, but only once every 18.6 years does it reach its true extremes of moonrise and moonset (known as major lunar standstills). Northern major moonrise is 4° north of midsummer solstice sunrise, and southern major moonrise is 6° south of midwinter solstice sunrise. The same goes for the relationship between major moonset and the midsummer and midwinter solstice sunsets.

The timing of major standstills is different from the solstice times of the year. However, the moon's rising and setting at its major standstills is most dramatic when the moon is full in midwinter or midsummer, approximately around the solstices. The southerly major moonrise and moonset coincide with full moon in midsummer, and the northerly major moonrise and moonset with full moon in midwinter.

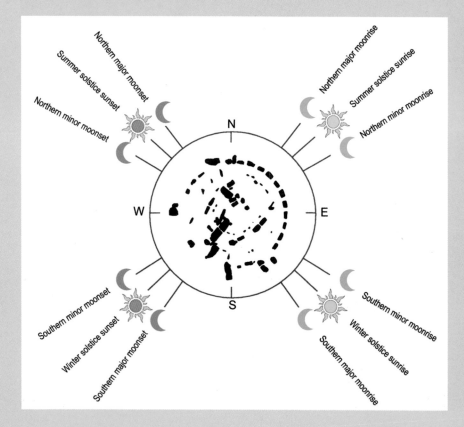

Figure 1.20
The directions of the solstices (sun) and standstills (moon) on the horizon for an observer in southern Britain (© Mike Parker Pearson)

The end of the Late Neolithic: Stonehenge stage 2, c 2500 BC

As we have seen, the first stage of Stonehenge was put up c 2900 BC, certainly before 2755 BC. It was used for cremation burials for about 600 years, but around the time that the practice of burying within Stonehenge was in decline, there was a major rebuilding of the monument. Radiocarbon dates on antler picks buried in the stone holes show that this took place at some point c 2500 BC. This date marks the end of the Late Neolithic, when Stonehenge took the form that largely survives today. At its centre were five sarsen trilithons – pairs of uprights with lintels. Hollows carved into the lintels fitted into protruding knobs on the tops of the sarsen uprights, similar to mortise and tenon joints in carpentry.

Figure 1.21 *The true scale of the sarsen trilithons can be seen in this photograph of the author, Mike Parker Pearson*

The largest of the five trilithons was the so-called 'great trilithon' on the south-west side, standing c 8m high and framing the setting of the sun at the midwinter solstice. This followed earlier instances of marking the midwinter solstice

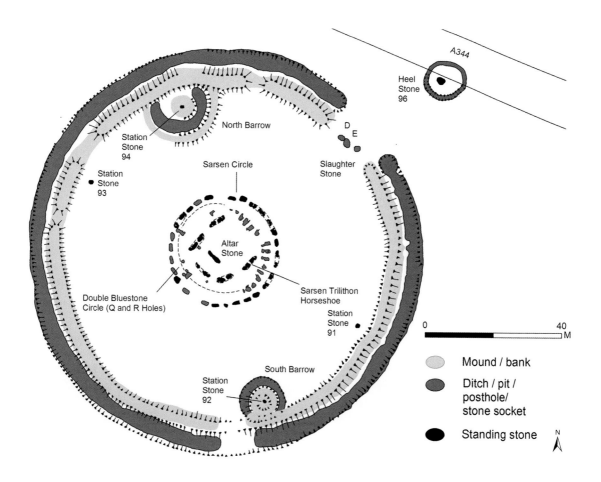

Understanding the monument

in the passage graves of Newgrange in Ireland and Maes Howe in Orkney. At Maes Howe, the setting midwinter sun shines down the tomb's entrance passage to illuminate the chamber. At Newgrange, a specially constructed 'light box' above the tomb's entrance allows the rising midwinter sun to shine along the passage and into the burial chamber. It seems that this association between the midwinter sun and the ancestors linked them with the darkest time of the year and the eternal cycling of time.

In stage 2, the bluestones were moved from their original arrangement (in a single ring just inside the ditch) and re-erected around the sarsen trilithons in a formation known as the Q and R Holes. They formed a double arc, pierced by an entrance at the north-east. There is no evidence that this double arc of bluestones

Figure 1.22
Stonehenge stage 2, c 2500 BC; the stones are erected in the centre of the interior (© Antiquity Publications Ltd. From Darvill et al 2012, drawn by Vanessa Constant)

Figure 1.23 The centre of Stonehenge was designed to be an enclosed space, with the stones positioned such that it is difficult for anyone outside the circle to see what is happening within the centre of the monument. In this photograph, taken in 2013, the positions of missing stones can be seen as parchmarks in the grass

continued in a full circle around the trilithons, and there may have been only a single row of stones (or perhaps none at all) to the south-west. It is possible that two bluestone lintels were set up in this period, one of them as part of the north-east entrance through the Q and R Holes. Outside this double arc of bluestones, the 30 upright stones of the sarsen circle were erected. Of these, seventeen still stand, nine are fallen and four are missing. The uprights were joined by lintels; only seven of the circle's original 30 sarsen lintels survive. The woodworking metaphor of mortise and tenon joints for attaching lintels to the tops of uprights was extended to dovetailed jointing fitting together the lintels' convex and concave ends around the sarsen circle.

Outside the sarsen circle, further arrangements of sarsen stones were probably put up at this time. Four small sarsens, known as the Station Stones, were positioned immediately inside the encircling bank: they formed a large rectangle, with two sides aligned towards midsummer sunrise in one direction and towards midwinter sunset in the other. The other two sides were oriented towards the southernmost point at which the moon rises (southern major moonrise) and the northernmost point

at which the moon sets (northern major moonset). Two of the Station Stones were enclosed by small structures, known as the south and north barrows. The south barrow was a low chalk mound constructed on a chalk plaster surface. This surface may have been the floor of a building that stood just inside the south entrance to Stonehenge's enclosure, before the barrow was built on top of it. Immediately inside the north-east entrance, the now-fallen Slaughter Stone was part of a façade of three upright stones across the entrance to Stonehenge. Its dramatic name is a product of pre-Victorian imagination and there is no evidence at all for its use in sacrifice. Finally, the Heel Stone may have been moved to its present position from a stone-hole immediately north-west of where it stands today.

A recent laser-scan examination of all the stones at Stonehenge has shown that the uprights of the sarsen circle were dressed slightly differently to those of the trilithons, suggesting that

Figure 1.24
It is clear that the monument was built to be viewed from the north-east, the direction from which the later Avenue approaches it

there may have been a time gap between the construction of the trilithons and the erection of the sarsen circle. There has been speculation in modern times about whether the stone circle was ever finished since some of the uprights are missing. We know that at least one sarsen has been taken away because archaeologists have found the hole where it once stood. Other holes for missing stones were noticed in 2013 when their locations were revealed by parch-marks in the grass, caused by a period of drought.

It is clear that in the last 2000 years many of Stonehenge's stones have been chipped away at, broken and removed either for use as building stone or as souvenirs. Results of the laser-scan study suggest that Stonehenge's sarsen circle probably was completed, but the south-west half of the sarsen circle was not as well built as the north-east half. It seems Stonehenge was built to be appreciated best when viewed from the north-east or from its centre.

The Copper Age: Stonehenge stage 3, c 2400 BC

Metalworking was a new technology that did not arrive in Britain until c 2500 BC. Although widespread in central and eastern Europe before 3000 BC, it did not reach Britain until at least 500 years later. Experts are unsure about when the use of metals reached coastal Europe but it seems likely that there was some initial resistance to copper and gold in the megalithic heartlands – including some Continental communities as well as Britain.

Around or soon after 2450 BC people in Britain adopted a new burial rite that was already widespread in northern and central Europe. This saw a change from cremation to inhumation burial in single graves with a style of decorated pot known as a Bell Beaker. Like metalworking, Bell Beakers originated in Europe and only spread to Britain some centuries after they first became common on the Continent. Other grave goods (objects placed in the grave) might include copper knives, gold hair-ornaments, beads, tools and flint arrowheads. The most lavishly provisioned grave from this period is that of the Amesbury Archer, who was buried at Boscombe Down, 3 miles (4.8km) south-east of Stonehenge. Chemical analysis of his teeth indicates that he grew up in continental Europe, as did a small proportion of the other

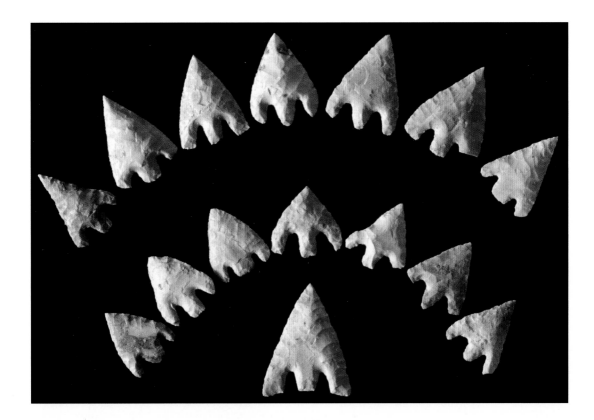

people buried with this new, foreign burial rite. The introduction of European influences brought to an end over a thousand years of isolation for the people of southern Britain.

To the north of Stonehenge, there was a final burst of large-scale monument-building with the construction of three enormous, conical, stepped chalk pyramids at Marlborough, Marden and Avebury. Silbury Hill at Avebury was the largest, requiring one million hours of hard labour. Despite archaeologists' best attempts to explore the mound, Silbury Hill has not yielded up the secret of why it was built. No burial has ever been found but we do know that it was originally a small barrow. We also know that the enormous mound was raised *c* 2400 BC, just as the Bell Beaker burial rite was becoming common practice in Britain. These three giant mounds represent the end of the large-scale mobilisation of thousands of people working to a single goal. From then on, monument-building was to be mostly small-scale, carried out at the level of families and lineages rather than entire tribes.

It might be assumed that the arrival from the Continent of Bell Beaker people, bringing with them knowledge of metallurgy and

Figure 1.25 *The superb collection of barbed and tanged arrowheads from the grave of the Amesbury Archer. One of the richest Beaker burials ever found in Europe, the grave contained a variety of objects including five Beakers, three copper knives, gold jewellery and a collection of archery equipment (© Wessex Archaeology)*

Figure 1.26 *Silbury Hill, near Avebury. Built c 2400 BC, extensive excavations in the 1960s and in 2007 failed to establish its purpose*

probably the wheel, was a time of bloodshed and ethnic violence. Yet, of the hundreds of burials from this period, only a handful of skeletons show signs of violence. This is a very different picture from earlier times: during the 4th millennium BC almost 7% of the skulls from burials have injuries inflicted by blows from wooden clubs, and other individuals have evidence that they were shot by arrows. Intriguingly, one of the very few victims of violent death in the Copper Age was buried at Stonehenge. Whereas all previous burials at Stonehenge had been cremations, this was a Bell Beaker-style inhumation, the dead man being laid in a grave dug into Stonehenge's outer ditch. Unusually, he was not provided with a Bell Beaker; his only grave good was an archer's wristguard but his grave contained three flint arrowheads – he had been shot. The arrowheads had lodged in his body cavity, damaging some of his bones on entry. From this impact damage, it was possible to establish that the arrows had pierced him on different sides of his body. His identity and why he was killed are a mystery: we know that he was a local man but why was he shot three times, from different directions? Was this an execution, an assassination, or a death in combat? His death is less likely to have been a sacrifice or a murder because he was buried with care in the conventional manner, lying on his left side. His burial may have been a continuation of previous rites at Stonehenge as many cremation burials had previously been put in the ditch.

Only minor architectural modifications were made in this period (stage 3) at Stonehenge. While the stone circle itself was not altered much, someone built a route towards the north-east entrance – the Stonehenge Avenue – which runs for 1¾ miles (2.8km) from Bluestonehenge beside the river at West Amesbury. At this time, the emptied holes of Bluestonehenge were

Figure 1.27
Stonehenge stage 3, c 2400 BC; the Avenue is constructed and minor alterations are made to the arrangement of the stones (© Antiquity Publications Ltd. From Darvill et al 2012, drawn by Vanessa Constant)

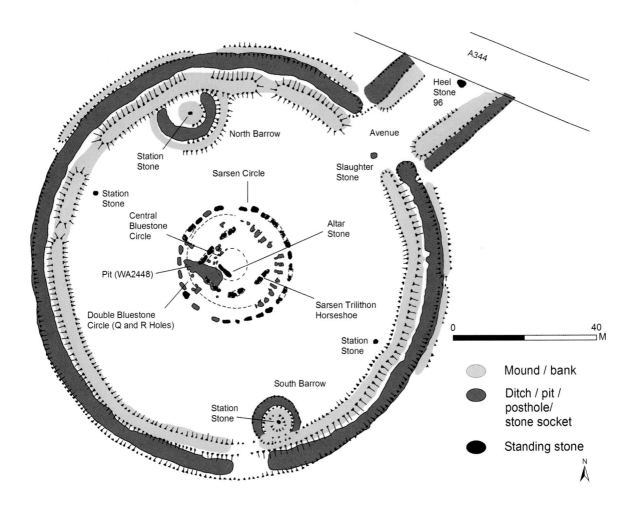

Figure 1.28 *A reconstruction of the monument in stages 2–3 (© Peter Dunn)*

enclosed within a small henge some 30m across, set into the riverside end of the Avenue. The Stonehenge Avenue consists of parallel ditches some 20m apart with low banks of chalk piled up inside the line of the ditches as well as probably outside them. The enclosing ditch at Stonehenge was also partially cleaned out at this time.

Understanding the monument

Whilst the Q and R Hole setting inside the sarsen circle remained in place, there may have been a new setting of bluestones added to the centre, in the form of an inner bluestone circle – very possibly the 25 or so bluestones of Bluestonehenge that were dismantled at this time beside the river at West Amesbury. Two of the three large sarsen uprights that had blocked the north-east entrance of Stonehenge's enclosure were taken down, leaving the third – the Slaughter Stone – still upright and in place. The south-west part of the inner bluestone circle was later cut into by a large and deep pit, dug against the base of the great trilithon. Just why this pit was dug is a mystery but it destabilised the trilithon's uprights so much that one collapsed and broke at some later, but unknown, point in time.

Figure 1.29
Excavations in progress at the site of Bluestonehenge, near West Amesbury. The people are standing in the excavated holes of the stones

The Early Bronze Age: Stonehenge stage 4, c 2100 BC

Figure 1.30
Stonehenge stage 4, c 2100 BC; the bluestones are rearranged within the sarsen circle (© Antiquity Publications Ltd. From Darvill et al 2012, drawn by Vanessa Constant)

From around 2300–2200 BC, people learned to alloy copper with tin to make bronze. Bronze is a much better metal than copper for making tools and weapons, and in Britain there were plentiful sources of tin in Cornwall. The people of Wessex benefited from their control of trade along the south coast to northern France and were able to obtain precious materials such as amber from the Baltic, jet from Whitby and gold from Ireland.

In this period people began to construct hundreds of round barrows (mounds containing the remains of the dead) on the land surrounding Stonehenge. Initially these were small, simple mounds with single burials under them, mostly of men rather than women, but after 2100 BC certain families built larger

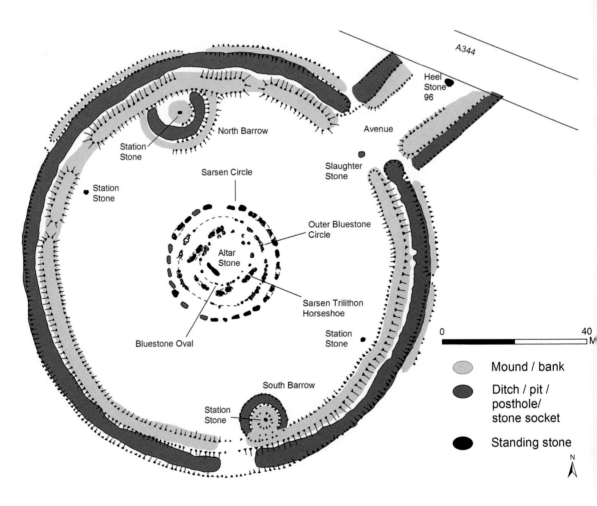

Figure 1.31 *A beautiful gold lozenge from the Bush Barrow burial mound. Made of thin sheet gold and measuring 18 x 15cm, the lozenge was probably once mounted on a wooden board and held in place by pins. It was placed on the man's chest in the grave (© Wiltshire Museum, Devizes)*

mounds that were often renewed and then enlarged. These large barrows contained the burials of men, women and children. After this fourth stage of Stonehenge, from about 1900 BC, we find important men and women being buried with substantial wealth in round barrows, many of them within sight of Stonehenge. The most impressive of these burials is that of the man buried beneath Bush Barrow, half a mile (0.8km) south of Stonehenge. His grave goods included two large bronze daggers, a ceremonial stone mace, a bronze axe, two gold lozenges and a gold belt-fastener.

At Stonehenge itself during this stage (*c* 2100 BC) the bluestones were entirely rearranged into a circle inside the ring of sarsens; inside that circle, further bluestones were arranged in an oval, inside the horseshoe of the trilithons. At some later point, as yet undated, the bluestones at the north-east end of this oval were removed to create a horseshoe-shaped array of stones, mirroring the plan of the sarsen trilithons. In addition, the ditches of the Avenue were cleaned out in this period. There are hints that, from this date onwards, several of the bluestones were broken up and the fragments made into stone tools, including hammerstones, a mace-head and a battle-axe. Many such items have been found amongst surface scatters of Early Bronze Age artefacts in various parts of the surrounding landscape, while others were deposited in graves or simply left, half-finished, at Stonehenge.

The Middle Bronze Age: Stonehenge stage 5, c 1600 BC

Figure 1.32
Stonehenge stage 5, c 1600 BC; the Y and Z holes are dug around the sarsen circle and over 100 carvings of axes are made on some of the stones (© Antiquity Publications Ltd. From Darvill et al 2012, drawn by Vanessa Constant)

There was a period of about 500 years after *c* 2100 BC when nothing much appears to have happened at Stonehenge. However, it then had a new lease of life with carvings being made on some of the stones and two concentric rings of pits being dug around the outside of the sarsen circle. Shortly after this, *c* 1500 BC, we see an agricultural revolution occurring in Britain: for the very first time, people divided up their common grazing land into field plots with visible boundaries – parallel sets of long ditches known as co-axial field systems. Farming practices which had previously been predominantly mobile and pastoralist (dependent on livestock) now switched to a more evenly balanced mix of pasture and cultivation. People were now more rooted to place in life; in

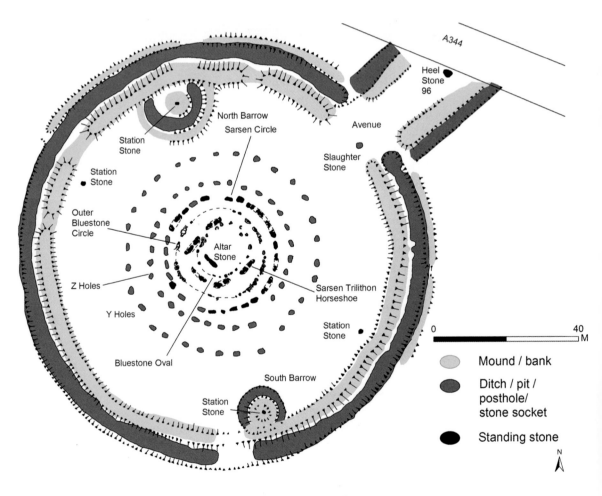

Figure 1.33 *Three large Bronze Age round barrows situated to the north-west of Stonehenge. By 1500 BC the landscape around Stonehenge was one of fields interspersed with numerous round barrows*

previous periods they had been rooted only in death, their lives having been highly mobile.

Up until 1500 BC the landscape around Stonehenge continued to fill up with round barrows, becoming an extensive cemetery that stretched for miles on both sides of the River Avon. The agricultural revolution had a profound effect on the Stonehenge landscape: as field boundaries were laid out, Stonehenge was left isolated within a plot of common land. Farms were built in amongst the fields and archaeologists have investigated the remains of one such farmstead and its field ditches, 400m west of Stonehenge. One of its field boundaries, known as the palisade ditch, runs to within 100m of Stonehenge itself.

Around this time two concentric circles of pits, known as the Y and Z Holes, were dug around the outside of the sarsen circle. No stones or wooden posts were ever erected in these pits, and nothing was placed in them; they were left to fill up naturally with soil. These pits may have been an abandoned attempt to rearrange the bluestones again, but their purpose remains mysterious. There appears to have been an entrance into the two concentric rings of Y and Z Holes on the south-east side because the spacing of pits is wide and uneven there. This was also the place where Middle Bronze Age pottery was most concentrated.

The only carvings on Stonehenge's stones date to this period, from *c* 1750 to 1500 BC: over 110 carvings of bronze axe-heads and four carvings of daggers (see Fig 5.3) were made on stones 3, 4 and 5 on the east side of the sarsen circle and on the south trilithon (stones 53 and 54). Elsewhere in Britain, carvings of axes and daggers from this period are mostly associated with burial places, and it is no coincidence that the area around Stonehenge has one of the largest and densest cemeteries of burial mounds (the round barrows) anywhere in Britain.

The Stonehenge landscape

The Stonehenge landscape

Salisbury Plain may seem an unlikely spot for a spectacular monument such as Stonehenge. The Plain is a plateau of rolling grass downland, with no great hills or outstanding natural landmarks. It was far from the attractive and sheltered valleys and lowlands where prehistoric farmers actually lived. The geology of the plain is chalk, the soft, white rock that, in southern England, extends in a broad ridge from the Thames valley in the north to the south coast. Chalk is highly porous so water does not remain on the surface: there are streams that issue from springs at the base of the chalk and rivers such as the Avon which have cut valleys through the chalk plateau. Stonehenge itself is over a mile (1.5km) from the nearest water source, the River Avon in its valley at Amesbury, and there are no lakes or natural ponds on the chalk downs. So why was Stonehenge built where it was? Archaeologists have begun to find an answer but it is not simple; it depends, among other things, on our understanding of long-term changes in vegetation and environment.

After the retreat of the glaciers at the end of the last Ice Age, c 17,000 years ago, plants and trees slowly colonised the land. As the climate warmed, so cold-loving species such as pine and birch were gradually replaced by oak, hazel and other deciduous species. Hunter-gatherers re-colonised Britain c 14,700 years ago when it was a tundra-like environment similar to that of northern Canada or Siberia today. By the time that Early Mesolithic people were putting up pine posts at Stonehenge some 10,000 years ago, the climate had become slightly warmer, equivalent to central Scandinavia today. This climatic period is known as the Boreal.

Figure 2.1 *(facing page) The view north across Woodhenge and Durrington Walls*

Botanists and climatologists have generally thought that Britain was covered in dense forest during the Mesolithic period, certainly by 6500 BC when it became an island separated from continental Europe. But recent studies of the ancient vegetation of Salisbury Plain and other high chalklands of Wessex have shown that the full succession of woodland species was slow and incomplete on these waterless chalk downs. Instead, trees on the high chalk grew only singly or in small stands or copses, leaving large areas of open grassland. An equivalent today would be the parkland landscapes of English stately homes, with trees and shrubs dotted across grassland.

Mesolithic hunter-gatherers lived in the forested valleys of the Thames and the Avon and their tributaries, and they must have found the open woodland of Salisbury Plain's chalk downs an ideal hunting-ground for stalking the large wild cattle, red deer and wild pigs that grazed on its grasslands and drank at freshwater pools along the river banks, such as Blick Mead. But with the advent of farming c 4000 BC came increased clearance of forest from valleys and high ground. Within the next thousand years, what little woodland there was on Salisbury Plain was almost entirely gone except in the valley bottoms. Stonehenge was built in a landscape that was probably even more open than it is today, the herds of cattle and sheep which periodically grazed these rich grasslands preventing scrub and woodland from regenerating.

A sacred place?

One of the big mysteries for archaeologists is why Early Mesolithic hunter-gatherers put up a line of huge wooden posts here on Salisbury Plain, and why so close to what was to become the site of Stonehenge. The new discovery of the long-lived seasonal gathering-site or home base at Blick Mead provides part of an answer because it means that large numbers of people were periodically gathered in one place in sufficient numbers to provide the labour required to erect these massive tree trunks at Stonehenge: they were probably at least 6m long and 1m in diameter. These pine posts were clearly more than just a signpost for directions to the Mesolithic campsite; such monuments are so unusual among hunter-gatherers anywhere in the world, past and present, that there must have been a special reason why they were put up here. A possible explanation was discovered in 2008 when we excavated a trench across the Stonehenge Avenue, the solstice-

Reconstructing past environments

Archaeologists study a variety of remains to work out what ancient environments looked like and how and when they changed. Ancient pollen is often preserved in wet deposits such as accumulations of silt within river channels. By taking samples at close intervals down a core extracted from a deep accumulation of river deposits, palynologists (experts who study pollen) can identify the different species of trees, shrubs and grasses, and establish the different proportions of these, to work out how densely the landscape was forested. By comparing each level with another down the core, they can see how certain species became more common than others. Early Neolithic landscapes in Britain tend to show a gradual reduction of oak and hazel woodland and an increase in grass species, resulting from increased grazing and the felling of trees.

Pollen can be blown long distances or, in the case of river deposits, washed some distance downstream. As a result, pollen diagrams give a broad-brush picture of the vegetation in the wider vicinity of around 30 or 40 miles (50–65km). A more precise and localised picture can be built up from the analysis of snails within buried deposits. Some species of snails are able

to live in several different environments but others are restricted to particular ecological niches. For example, some species live only in damp and shady woodland while others are found only in open, well-grazed grassland or even periodically grazed grassland. The vast majority of these niche-specific snails are too small to be picked out by the naked eye; block samples of soil must be taken and then sieved through very fine mesh to recover the snails, which are then identified under a microscope. In the Stonehenge area, snails from buried soils beneath burial mounds and in other locations have shown that there was much more grassland during the Neolithic than was once thought.

Figure 2.2 *A selection of snails commonly found in archaeological deposits, with typical habitats. Clockwise from top:* Vallonia costata – *open country;* Pupilla muscorum – *open short grassland and bare soil;* Punctum pygmaeum – *shady woodland and rough grassland;* Clausilia bidentata – *fallen timber and leaf litter.* Clausilia *is 9–10mm in length* (© Mike Allen)

Figure 2.3
Excavations across the Avenue, showing the periglacial features in the centre and the ditches on either side. The line of the Avenue can be seen running away to the north-east

aligned ceremonial access that leads to Stonehenge's north-east entrance.

What we found was a series of deep, narrow channels in the chalk, running along the centre of the Avenue, parallel with its solstice axis. Expecting these features to be artificial – surely only something man-made could have such an alignment – we were amazed to discover that the channels in the chalk bedrock were, in fact, naturally formed in a previous Ice Age as periglacial fissures that were filled with fine chalk-derived sediment many thousands of years before any human hunters arrived here. Periglacial fissures form during long periods of intense freezing and thawing as water flows downhill. The reason for such large fissures forming here was that water had been channelled between two naturally formed parallel chalk ridges, also, by complete chance, on the solstice axis.

Today, these parallel chalk ridges are just visible along the line of the banks of the Stonehenge Avenue, running for *c* 150m north-east from the Heel Stone, but the fissures cannot be seen on the surface because of the depth of soil covering them. However, they may have caught the attention of hunters 10,000 years ago – in

The Stonehenge landscape

dry weather, as the grass became parched on what was then a very thin post-glacial soil, the fissures would have shown up as coloured stripes. The ridges would also have been much more prominent than they are today, before 10,000 years of weathering. Similar periglacial stripes can be seen today as vegetation marks next to the site of the Neolithic flint mines at Grimes Graves, Norfolk.

Perhaps the pine posts were placed in the vicinity of the periglacial feature to mark this place as a special conjunction of cosmological elements, the marks in the land pointing towards the sun's extreme positions of midwinter solstice sunset and midsummer solstice sunrise. Both are important moments in the calendar of modern-day hunter-gatherers in the circumpolar regions of the northern hemisphere. Such a place where the heavens and the earth came together might have been considered an *axis mundi*, an axis or centre of the world. The camp at Blick Mead may have been far more than just a handy place to gather, but somewhere that people returned to as a place of origin. Over the centuries and millennia that it was used, this place would have become the centre of a network of paths leading towards it from many parts of southern Britain. Just as all roads led to Rome, so all these paths led to the future site of Stonehenge.

Farmers in the landscape

We don't know if people retained knowledge of this special place across the transition to agriculture. Farmers use land in very different ways to hunter-gatherers: time-scheduling and seasonal labour mobilisation become crucial. Yet many aspects of the previous lifestyle of hunting and gathering continued, even after the introduction to Britain of domesticated animals and crops. Wild foods (but curiously not marine foods) still formed a major part of the diet, and settlements were small and dispersed. There were no villages, just hamlets or single houses, and people probably continued to be mobile during the annual round. Farming needs boundaries and ownership and is therefore prone to disputes over cattle, crops and territory. Such disputes can boil over into violence that may need to be dealt with by holding gatherings where grievances are heard, arguments settled, and alliances formed. People may have gathered together for such reasons at the causewayed enclosures and other monuments built during the Early and Middle Neolithic. These sites were

Figure 2.4
Unlike many other monuments, Stonehenge is not a prominent feature in the landscape. This is the view east-north-east towards Beacon Hill ridge

once thought to be settlements but, now that many have been excavated, it is clear that they were occupied only occasionally and used for activities such as feasting and the exchange of tools and pottery.

The Coneybury pit, Robin Hood's Ball causewayed enclosure and the two Stonehenge cursus monuments tell us where such intermittent gatherings of people, in their hundreds and thousands, took place on Salisbury Plain in the Early and Middle Neolithic (during the 4th millennium BC). The monument-building of that era is also testament to the sacred or religious significance of this area: Robin Hood's Ball is positioned with views towards the site of Stonehenge, as is Coneybury, whilst the Greater Cursus blocks off the Stonehenge area from the land to its north. Yet the Stonehenge area was only one of many landscapes across Britain that became ceremonial complexes after 3800 BC. Causewayed enclosures, the majority of which are found south of the River Trent, are usually located about 25 miles (40km) apart or even closer, forming ceremonial centres for a population that, in its daily life, lived dispersed across southern Britain. The same is true for cursus monuments. The Stonehenge area in 3800–3000 BC seems not to have been any more special than any other monument complex in the region. If anything, it was a bit behind the times as no long barrows or other such tombs have been found which date to before 3600 BC.

Neolithic monuments and sites in Wessex and the Thames valley

To understand Stonehenge in its landscape, archaeologists have to treat it as part of a wider region that changed through time. Stonehenge and other henges in southern England were the successors of Early Neolithic causewayed enclosures in terms of locational continuity and their role as gathering places for large numbers of people. Causewayed enclosures, built c 3800–3600 BC in Wessex and the Thames valley, were located on the edges of groups of long barrows that probably defined different social territories. In addition, there appears to have been a major territorial boundary running north–south from the Wash to the south coast, marked by a dense spread of causewayed enclosures. Robin Hood's Ball, the causewayed enclosure closest to Stonehenge, lies within this spread. On either side of this divide there are noticeable differences in the material culture and funerary architecture of the time. It is possible, therefore, that causewayed enclosures were built in these places because of their role in enabling gatherings and resolving conflict between different territorial groups.

Middle Neolithic cursus monuments (c 3600–3200 BC) are found in similar locations to causewayed enclosures, especially along major rivers where they often mark off a large plot of land bounded by water on other sides. There are fewer cursus monuments than causewayed enclosures, especially in the Thames valley. One of the major ceremonial complexes, at Avebury, is unusual in having a causewayed enclosure and a henge but no cursus. The distribution of cursus monuments and, after them, henges, shows a marked shift to the east. This may indicate the encroachment of different groups of people expanding out of their original territories from the west.

Late Neolithic henges are found in similar localities to cursus monuments within Wessex and the Thames valley. They are often located at significant points along rivers or near to their sources.

Figure 2.5 *The stone circle at Avebury, enclosed within its large bank*

Archaeologists often call these monument complexes 'central places' – prehistoric equivalents of towns, in contrast to villages and hamlets – but they were, in all likelihood, 'peripheral' or even 'neutral' places located on the boundaries between populations or territories, as well as on natural routeways between settlement areas. The distribution of long barrows is one indicator of such territories: Robin Hood's Ball and other causewayed enclosures in Wessex lie on the edges of these groups of tombs. No-one actually lived full-time on top of the chalk: people farmed the valleys and lowlands on either side of Salisbury Plain. The Plain, and indeed the entire chalk plateau running from Avebury in the north to Dorchester in Dorset in the south, was a boundary area for farming groups: it was used for grazing on the high grasslands and for large-scale gatherings to meet people from the 'other side of the hill'.

Stonehenge in the landscape

Even when Stonehenge was first built *c* 2900 BC, the landscape around it was crowded with a palimpsest of monuments and long-visited places. This was already an ancient place with a human imprint that stretched back 5000 years. This first Stonehenge was a circular enclosure reserved for cremation burials, with standing stones and posts. It is probable that Welsh bluestone pillars were set in the 56 Aubrey Holes to form a large stone circle within the banks of the enclosure (see Fig 1.14). Special offerings of cattle skulls and other animal bones were also placed in the bottom of its ditch. There was something very special about why these particular bones were buried. We know from radiocarbon-dating that some of them were already 200 years old when they were put in the ground and we also know that one of these cattle was raised in western Britain, quite possibly from the same region in which the bluestones originated. At around this time the smaller circle known as Bluestonehenge, consisting of some 25 or so bluestones, was erected a mile away at the riverside in West Amesbury, but no cremated remains were found at this former stone circle.

The choice of location for the Stonehenge cremation enclosure might have been influenced by the periglacial ridges and fissures, since the south-west end of this natural feature led directly into the enclosure's main entrance. In other words, anyone approaching the enclosure from the north followed a 150m-long natural 'avenue' oriented in the direction of the midwinter solstice sunset.

The centre of Stonehenge has been heavily disturbed by people digging there over many centuries so it is difficult to know whether something special was located here. However, there are hints that this may not have been a 'greenfield' site. The so-called 'north barrow' within the enclosure could have been an earlier, smaller enclosure cut into by the enclosure's ditch. There is also a low mound just south-east of the centre of Stonehenge; part of its edge was revealed during excavations in 2008, and it appears to be a natural mound of some sort. Intriguingly, a loose piece of charcoal found in that excavation produced a radiocarbon date of the same age as the Early Mesolithic posts.

Just where the builders of this first Stonehenge lived is unknown. One possible location is Wilsford Down, south-west of Stonehenge, where finds of pottery and arrowheads of this date have been found on the ground surface. Another possibility is

Figure 2.6 *A reconstruction of the stone circle at Bluestonehenge, on the banks of the Avon at West Amesbury (© Peter Dunn)*

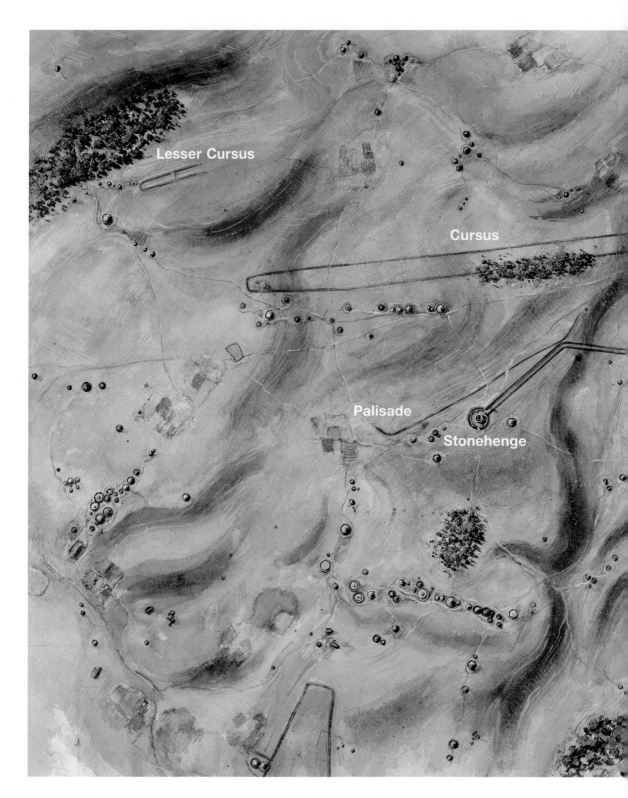

The Stonehenge landscape

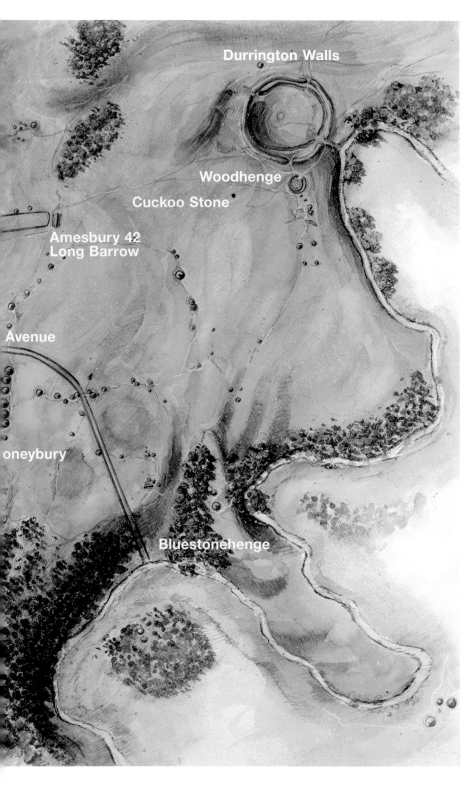

Durrington Walls

Woodhenge

Cuckoo Stone

Amesbury 42
Long Barrow

Avenue

oneybury

Bluestonehenge

Figure 2.7 *The Stonehenge landscape c 1600 BC (© Historic England)*

Figure 2.8 *Chisel arrowhead found during excavations at Bluestonehenge*

the valley that runs from Coneybury to West Amesbury where Bluestonehenge is located. Coneybury lies on a long ridge halfway between Stonehenge and West Amesbury. Many chisel arrowheads of this period have been found here during fieldwalking and there is also a partially excavated structure at Coneybury that dates to around this time. This consists of a group of pits that are of a size consistent with having once held large wooden posts in a rectangular arrangement, surrounded by wooden stakes. This timber structure is too large to have been a house and was most likely a monument of some sort; it was later enclosed by a bank and ditch as a classic henge.

The Stonehenge landscape

Stonehenge and Durrington Walls

Around 2500 BC, at the very end of the Neolithic period, Stonehenge received a massive make-over. Some 80 large blocks of sarsen were brought to the site, probably from the Marlborough Downs, 20 miles (32km) to the north, to join the 80 or so bluestones. The large sarsen stones were probably shaped to approximate size in the as-yet undiscovered hollows where they lay. They were later dressed using sarsen hammerstones outside the Stonehenge enclosure, to its north (see Fig 4.17). They were then taken into the enclosure and erected as the inner horseshoe of trilithons and the outer circle of uprights and lintels.

The question of where the builders lived had been a puzzle for many years until we discovered the remains of a large but short-lived settlement beneath the banks of the nearby henge at Durrington Walls. Before the excavations at Durrington Walls between 2004 and 2007, archaeologists had failed to find any trace of Late Neolithic settlement in the immediate vicinity of Stonehenge other than scatters of flint arrowheads and a few stone tools. Excavations within Stonehenge and in close proximity to it had failed to find the quantities of Grooved Ware pottery, animal bones and other residues of daily life that would have been left behind by the substantial workforce needed to build the stone circle at Stonehenge (in its second stage).

Durrington Walls is almost 2 miles (3.2km) from Stonehenge, in a dry valley that meets the River Avon north of Amesbury. With a diameter of 440m, it is Britain's largest henge. Outside its south entrance lies Woodhenge, a small henge built around a timber circle. Two more timber circles lay within Durrington Walls: the Southern Circle and the smaller Northern Circle. Woodhenge was excavated in 1928 and the two Durrington Walls timber circles were dug in 1967, but it was only in 2004–07 that remains were found underneath the henge's banks of a large village, around the wooden circles. Since the remains of the village were beneath the banks of the henge, we know that the village was there before the henge was built.

Thanks to new, more precise methods of radiocarbon-dating, Durrington Walls henge can be dated to 2480–2460 BC. The village beneath the henge was occupied for no more than 55 years in the period *c* 2500 BC. For exactly how long we cannot be sure but it may have been no more than a decade. All of the houses in the village appear to have been lived in at the same time: none was built on top of an earlier house. Each house had a floor of

Figure 2.9
Woodhenge, situated just to the south of Durrington Walls, was first excavated by Maud Cunnington in the 1920s. The site consists of six concentric oval rings of posts surrounded by a ditch and an outer bank. It measures 110m across, with a single entrance to the north-east. A small number of postholes were re-excavated by the Stonehenge Riverside Project team in 2008

smoothed chalk plaster which, in some cases, had been applied many times: in one house the floor had been re-plastered as many as seven times. Similarly, each house had a group of pits outside it that had provided the chalk slurry from which to make floor plaster and also the chalk daub to cover and repair the walls. In one group, there were twelve pits, each dug into the edge of the one before. If repairs to floors and walls had taken place on, say, an annual cycle, just a decade or two might be a good guess for how long the village was inhabited. If Durrington Walls was indeed the camp where the builders of Stonehenge stage 2 lived, then it is likely that this stage of Stonehenge was built within a decade. This may seem like a long time for a single construction, given the thousands of people involved, but, as explained below, building work may have been concentrated seasonally in the autumn and winter months rather than occurring all year round.

Although only nine houses were excavated at Durrington Walls, the density of Neolithic houses there is unparalleled anywhere else in Britain except Orkney. Extrapolating from the traces of occupation found beneath the henge bank around its circuit, it is likely that there were as many as 1000 houses, so we can estimate a likely population of 4000 people or more. This equates to the estimate of the number of people needed to dig Durrington Walls' huge, deep ditch a generation later. Most of the inhabitants of Durrington Walls probably did not live there all year round. Analysis of the season of death of the huge numbers of pigs consumed by the inhabitants has revealed that the vast majority of animals were slaughtered in the autumn and wintertime. This evidence for winter feasting coincides with Stonehenge's emphasis on the midwinter solstice sunset.

Another link between Durrington Walls and Stonehenge is the orientation of the two timber circles within the Durrington Walls settlement. They both have solstitial orientations: their entrances face towards the midwinter solstice sunrise. From the riverside an

Figure 2.10 *Plan of Woodhenge and Durrington Walls, with the avenue running south-east towards the River Avon (© Irene de Luis)*

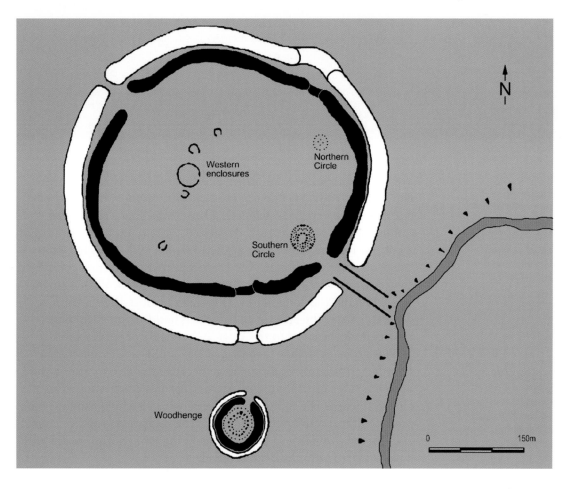

Figure 2.11
Excavations in progress at the eastern end of the Durrington Walls avenue and surrounding settlement

Figure 2.12 *(facing page) A ripple-flaked arrowhead found during the excavations at West Amesbury (Avenue ditch). Length: 45mm*

avenue leads 170m to the larger Southern Circle. Not only is this Durrington Walls avenue oriented on midsummer solstice sunset but its original surface (beneath a later, man-made surface of rammed flint) was naturally deposited. This is another instance of a natural feature aligned on a solstitial axis and appropriated by the people of Stonehenge. The Durrington Walls avenue connected the Southern Circle to the bank of the River Avon. With a surface 15m wide and flanking banks, this was far more than a track to get water from the river. A house-sized building on each bank provided views down to the river, presumably of processions.

We can be sure that this avenue was a link not simply to the river but ultimately to Stonehenge because the two locations were opposite sides of the same coin. Durrington's Southern Circle looked towards the midwinter solstice sunrise whilst Stonehenge's great trilithon was oriented towards the midwinter solstice sunset. Durrington Walls was a place of the living whilst Stonehenge was a place where only the dead dwelled.

The Stonehenge landscape

It seems that this unusually meandering stretch of the River Avon, between Durrington and West Amesbury, had a special significance as a physical and perhaps even supernatural link to Stonehenge, winding its way through a small gorge and past Blick Mead. Downstream at West Amesbury, about 100 years later, people built the Stonehenge Avenue leading from the Avon to Stonehenge. While the ditches for this avenue were not dug until c 2400 BC, the construction of the bluestone circle known as Bluestonehenge at West Amesbury, which is thought to date to c 3000 BC, indicates that this was an important spot from early on.

It may seem curious that a prehistoric workforce should choose to live nearly 2 miles (3.2km) from their place of work – Stonehenge – but the construction of the stone circle was much more than an ordinary building project. Stonehenge was a place of the dead, full of cremation deposits, so keeping a healthy distance between the living and the dead might well have seemed sensible for the living. Similar distancing of the dead from the living at this time has been noted elsewhere in Britain. For example, two Late Neolithic enclosures have been found near Perth in Scotland. One of these, at Forteviot, is associated with cremated human remains and the sockets of removed standing stones. The other, 2 miles (3.2km) upstream at Leadketty, is associated with settlement debris including large quantities of Grooved Ware. In Orkney, the Ring of Brodgar stone circle lies a mile (1.5km) to the north of a large settlement at the Ness of Brodgar, located on a long, thin peninsula. This concern with putting distance between the dead and the living was probably widespread across Britain in the 3rd millennium BC.

The Durrington Walls houses

Excavations at Durrington Walls in 2004–07 revealed the remains of nine houses dating to c 2500 BC. Seven of these were located beneath the east entrance of the henge, and two were set within their own ditched enclosures (known as the Western Enclosures) in the centre of the henge. The houses at the east entrance had well-preserved floors covered with domestic debris left behind when each house was last used. The houses were square in plan (about 5.3m x 5.3m) with rounded corners. The interior of each house was covered with a floor of chalk 'plaster', extending to within a metre of the walls. Various types of wooden furniture filled this zone around the edge, leaving postholes and beam-slots to show where

Figure 2.13 *Aerial view of one of the houses at Durrington Walls, showing the outer ring of stake holes and the floor of compacted chalk. Mike Parker Pearson is kneeling in the indentations left by the occupants as they knelt by the central hearth*

box beds, shelving and storage spaces once stood. A central hearth was set in a sunken circular fireplace. The walls were made of wattle and daub and the house roofs were probably thatched with reeds from the nearby riverside. The house interiors would have been very like the interiors of Orcadian houses at Skara Brae. In Orkney the furniture survives because, in the absence of wood, it had to be built of stone.

The Durrington Walls houses show a wide range of differences, related both to social status and to different activities. The two houses excavated in the Western Enclosures were clearly special, inhabited by people either of a high status or with a special ritual role (or both – we cannot tell). One of the east entrance houses had its own outhouse and was separated by a fence from other nearby dwellings. Two 'houses' on the banks of the Durrington Walls avenue were not actual dwellings but were open on one side; this would have provided views along the avenue to the river, and they may have been used during ceremonies. The small, square Durrington Walls houses are of the sort that people lived in. Larger houses, built in a D-plan, were most likely meeting houses. The largest timber structures were, of course, the timber circles. Stonehenge is basically a stone version of a wooden meeting house in a timber circle.

Figure 2.14 *Stone-built furniture inside a reconstructed house at Skara Brae. The houses at Durrington Walls had similar furniture, but built of timber*

After Stonehenge: barrows in the landscape

These distinctions in the landscape between the places of the living and the places of the dead changed after 2400 BC as people started to use the land on either side of this stretch of the River Avon for their burial mounds. Gradually, over the next 900 years, the entire area on both sides of the river became a vast cemetery of round barrows. There are more than 670 Bronze Age barrows on this part of Salisbury Plain. Many of them are positioned so that Durrington Walls, not Stonehenge, is visible from them. That said, Stonehenge has an 'envelope' of unused land around the monument, with only 40 or so barrows close to the stones, but certain groups of barrows are visible on the horizon in all directions when looking outwards from Stonehenge.

The Stonehenge landscape contains the largest and almost the densest cluster of round barrows in Britain. An even denser, but smaller, cluster is found in Thanet in Kent and clusters are also found around other former henge complexes such as Avebury and Dorchester, but the Stonehenge barrows are the most remarkable. Not only is there a great variety of barrow forms in the Stonehenge area – bell, saucer, pond, bowl and disc – but many of the barrows were built in ways that seem to us unnecessarily laborious. When the great storm of 1987 blew down trees on top of barrows on King Barrow Ridge, north-east of Stonehenge, archaeologist Mike Allen discovered that these barrows were built not of chalk but of turf and topsoil. Each had been created by heaping up quantities of turf and soil, no doubt taken from the surrounding grassland, and thus building each barrow would have destroyed several hectares of agricultural land. Not only was this economically wasteful, but the back-breaking task would have been very little fun for the mourners, who would have dug up the turf with antler picks and other basic tools.

People were certainly living in this landscape as it filled up with round barrows. They left traces of their settlements to the west, north-west and north of Stonehenge, as well as on the other side of the river at Boscombe Down, east of Amesbury. Yet the area in between these two zones, south and east of Stonehenge and next to the river's west bank, seems not to have been settled. There is no obvious agricultural reason for this avoidance so it may be that there were religious and political prohibitions on living in certain places.

Stonehenge among fields

Round barrow building ended *c* 1500 BC. Stonehenge now became surrounded by a fully farmed landscape of bounded fields. One of the first field boundaries to be constructed, perhaps around the same time as the Y and Z Holes, was a timber palisade that ran north-east–south-west across the land to the west of Stonehenge. It seems to have reinforced the distinction between the settled areas to the west and north and the areas to the south and east where settlement was absent. The palisade ran for 2 miles (3.2km) but was not continuous: there was a 100m-wide gap within it to the north-west of Stonehenge, so it seems not to have been defensive or even capable of keeping people and animals out. Its timber posts were left to decay in some segments and removed in others, being replaced by an open ditch that was later cleaned out on several occasions. The ditch finally silted up *c* 1450 BC when a sheep was buried in it. The abandoned ditch was later used for human burials *c* 1200 BC (in the Late Bronze Age) and *c* 600 BC (in the Iron Age).

The palisade ditch, as it is called, seems not to have an entirely agricultural purpose. It delineated a block of land, 2.5 km x 1.4 km, that incorporated Stonehenge and the two most impressive groups of round barrows – those on Normanton Down and on King Barrow Ridge. Perhaps it formalised earlier links between Stonehenge and the families who now buried their dead in these prestigious groups of barrows. Whatever the reason, this land was set aside for grazing whilst the rest of the Stonehenge landscape was divided up into a patchwork of cultivated fields. In the succeeding millennia much of Stonehenge's landscape has been ploughed at one time or another. Today's grass cover, grazed by sheep, belies a long and active history of agricultural transformation.

Reconstruction paintings – how and why they are done

Creating a reconstruction painting is a complex process, involving site visits, research, and collaboration with archaeologists, historians and many other experts. After visiting the site and getting immersed in the subject, there is first a period of gathering information together – excavation reports, sketches, plans and photographs – and accessing ideas on the interpretation of the evidence and making sense of it yourself, before trying to come up with a reconstruction that will communicate all this to the viewer.

Next comes a simple rough sketch from the best viewpoint with basic details of the site; at this and each worked-up rough drawing there will be discussions over various points of detail. Sometimes this can take a while and the academic process is often cut short if the finished painting is needed to meet a deadline for a book or exhibition.

The aim of the reconstruction is to use available evidence and theories to create an interpretation that will inform and inspire people, from academics to young viewers, about particular aspects of the past. The results of archaeological excavations are often difficult to visualise when holes in the ground are all that is left of impressive oak posts, or plaster floors are all that survive of houses that have lost their walls and roofs. Landscapes can change

Figure 2.15 *Reconstruction artist Peter Dunn discussing details with Julian Thomas during the excavations at Bluestonehenge*

Figure 2.16 *Peter Dunn's draft pencil sketch of the houses at Durrington Walls; see Figure 2.17 for the finished painting (© Peter Dunn)*

dramatically over thousands of years, with soil moving downhill by erosion and cultivation, or the course of a river altering. There may be woodland where once there was open grassland, whilst modern buildings and roads can interfere with the view of the past.

The artist's task is to illustrate the interpretive leap so that we can all appreciate what was once there. The full range of evidence is needed, including the results of pollen analysis and other environmental studies, to bring the past alive, to get a feeling for how the world might have looked to the people of the ancient past, and how they themselves may have looked as they constructed and used sites such as Stonehenge and Durrington Walls.

Of course, no reconstruction can ever represent exactly what the past was like; there are many layers of interpretation and new evidence will change our understanding over the years. Decisions are made at every stage that can affect the view and details in the final painting; this will also reflect the artist's own vision and style. The purpose should always be the same: to create 'a sense of place' and to stimulate the viewer to look at the past and ask questions about what life was like hundreds or even thousands of years ago.

Figure 2.17
Houses at Durrington Walls – the finished painting (© Peter Dunn)

Stonehenge and society

Stonehenge 3
and society

Just why Stonehenge was built is a question that was first asked long before our modern age. The earliest attempt to answer it dates from almost 1000 years ago, written down by a monk called Geoffrey of Monmouth in his *History of the Kings of Britain* about AD 1136.

The story Geoffrey tells is that a group of Britons was treacherously slain by invading Saxons. To mark this massacre at Amesbury, the magician Merlin ordered the building of a stone monument to stand as a cenotaph for the dead. Merlin also decreed that the stones for this memorial should be brought from far away, from Mount Killaurus in Ireland, taking them from a stone circle previously erected by giants. The reason for this, claimed Merlin, was that the stones of this circle were magical and had healing powers. Merlin took 10,000 men to Ireland to bring back the stones and erected them at Stonehenge exactly as they had been arranged on Mount Killaurus (or so says Geoffrey).

We have no idea where Geoffrey heard the story or whether he simply made it up himself. Some people think romantically that it is a relic of prehistoric folk-memory rather than a medieval monk's attempt to explain an ancient mystery. But Geoffrey's story is riddled with inconsistencies and mistakes: Stonehenge is much older than the Saxons and Britons, who were fighting 700 years before Geoffrey; secondly, none of Stonehenge's stones comes from Ireland; and there never were any giants (or wizards, obviously!). Myths and legends may be fun to read but archaeology consistently debunks such stories, while always searching for any tiny grain of truth that may hide within.

Figure 3.1 *(facing page) Detail from Peter Dunn's imagining of a ceremony at Bluestonehenge. The figures are carrying artefacts of the kind recovered from excavations at Stonehenge: cattle skulls, a mace-head and a stone axe (© Peter Dunn)*

Are there any grains of truth in Geoffrey's story? Substitute Wales for Ireland and that could account for the bluestones, brought from far away. Calling Stonehenge a monument to the dead is also echoed by archaeological discoveries inside Stonehenge. Yet such similarities between Geoffrey's story and the hard facts could merely be chance coincidences. We need to put the story, enchanting though it is, to one side and examine the archaeological evidence. As shown in the previous chapters, archaeologists know a great deal about when Stonehenge was built and what it contained, as well as how it was sited within its wider landscape. To understand the society that built it we can draw upon architecture, geographical patterns of organisation and movement, portable artefacts and their decorations, people's diet and pathology, and burial practices.

Society before Stonehenge

Britain during the 4th millennium BC was a violent and divided island, judging by the injuries on skulls buried in tombs and causewayed enclosure ditches. Two causewayed enclosures, at Hambledon Hill in Dorset and Crickley Hill in Gloucestershire, show evidence of having been attacked c 3400 BC. There may have been full-scale warfare in parts of the south-west, extending into Devon and Cornwall.

The population of Britain was very small – perhaps fewer than 200,000 – and people lived a largely dispersed life in small, remote communities, only coming together occasionally to take part in large gatherings. At certain moments during the 4th millennium these gatherings involved the building and use of monuments such as causewayed enclosures and tombs. The world of the living was ephemeral and transient, whereas that of the dead was often monumental and fixed. Such Early Neolithic monuments required communal effort to build them but this was tiny in comparison to the labour later needed to build Stonehenge and other Late Neolithic monuments. A causewayed enclosure could be constructed by 1000 people or fewer within a single season, a long barrow by just a few hundred.

There are no material indications that Early Neolithic Britain was a class-based society: there may well have been leaders and elders but the communal burial rites, in which many people were interred together in the same tomb, project an ideology of relative equality. Long barrows and other burial monuments were built by

and for groups. Only after 3500 BC did large groups of people get together to build monuments for individuals.

The Middle Neolithic (3400–3000 BC) saw a change from communal to individual burial that hints at certain people now having considerable power over others. Although there was no gold or silver with which to bolster inequalities, the appearance at this time of individual graves with numerous grave goods and covered by large burial mounds reveals the rise of elites. One of these special graves is Liff's Low in Derbyshire where the dead man was provided with an antler mace-head, two tusks of wild boar, polished flint axes and knives, flint arrowheads and red ochre for body decoration. At Duggleby Howe in Yorkshire a succession of burials in a very large round barrow included some with similarly fancy grave goods. One man buried here appears to have been accompanied by a gruesome trophy – the head of a young woman who was clubbed on the side of her head at the time of her death.

Evidence for farming in the Middle Neolithic is hard to find,

Figure 3.2 *One of the fifteen layers of disarticulated human bones found in a pit at a circular, triple-ditched Neolithic enclosure at Banbury Lane, Northampton. The deposit contains the remains of at least 165 individuals and has been dated to the Middle Neolithic (3360–3100 BC) (© MOLA Northampton)*

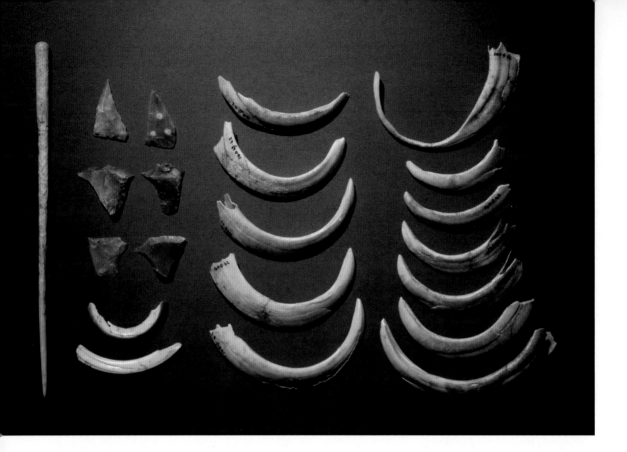

Figure 3.3 *The grave goods from Burial 7 at Duggleby Howe round barrow, East Yorkshire. The group includes six arrowheads, two beaver teeth chisels, a bone pin and twelve boars' tusks, some of which have been worked (© National Museums Scotland; courtesy of Hull Museums)*

as is any trace of the houses that people lived in. It may be that there was a change to increasing pastoralism, relying on animals rather than cereals. Overall, woodlands regenerated in this period as previously cleared areas of cultivation reverted to forest. Of course, some grassland areas such as Stonehenge were not affected by these vegetational changes.

Monument building switched to new styles of round barrow and cursuses. It is interesting that the Greater Stonehenge cursus and the long barrow at its east end were apparently built as a unit, linking certain of the dead directly to this prestigious and labour-consuming structure. Cursus monuments are not found on the Continent, in contrast to causewayed enclosures, long barrows and other Early Neolithic tombs which are found in Europe as well as Britain, and they represent the first fully indigenous monument form in Britain. The Greater Cursus at Stonehenge is a good-sized example, its construction requiring four times as much labour as Robin Hood's Ball, built a couple of centuries earlier. Not all cursus monuments required as much labour-power to build as the Greater Cursus; many were much smaller, just a few hundred metres long. In contrast, the largest is the Dorset Cursus on

Cranborne Chase, a massive 10 miles (16km) long. Even though the Dorset Cursus is actually two cursuses joined end to end, each of them is more than twice as long as the Stonehenge Greater Cursus.

The greatest investment in monument-building at this time was in Ireland, specifically at the Bend in the Boyne where the huge tombs of Knowth and Newgrange, built *c* 3200 BC, represent a new type of 'super monument'. The discovery of a very fine carved stone mace-head in one of the chambers at Knowth provides a further indication that people of power and authority were buried within these passage graves. These tombs required

Figure 3.4 *The southern cursus monument at Holywood, Dumfries and Galloway, showing clearly as a cropmark. The Holywood complex includes two cursus monuments and a stone circle (© RCAHMS)*

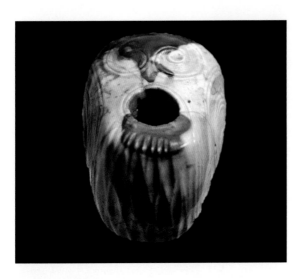

the labour of many hundreds if not thousands of people, to bring building materials such as quartz blocks from the Wicklow Mountains 40 miles (65km) to the south, and to construct the tomb. The building of such monuments would also have required enormous supplies of food for feeding the workers, as well as other resources such as ropes, timbers and antler picks. Years of planning would have been necessary to raise the herds of animals for eating, to collect all the raw materials, and to make the ropes and other equipment.

Figure 3.5 *The beautiful carved stone mace-head from Knowth, Ireland. Items such as this were clearly prestige objects and indicate that this was the tomb of a powerful person in Neolithic society (© Ken Williams)*

Stonehenge stage 1 – a circle for the dead, c 2900 BC

As explained earlier, the first stage of Stonehenge, built *c* 2900 BC, consisted of an enclosure for cremation burials, wooden posts and standing stones. Architecturally, it drew upon ideas developed not in southern England but in Ireland, Wales and Scotland. The concept of orientation on a solstice axis is a feature of Newgrange, where cremation burial was already practised. Stonehenge is a late example of a 'formative' henge, one of the earliest being at Llandygai in north Wales. At Stonehenge, cremated human remains were used in the packing to hold up standing stones (in the Aubrey Holes), and this practice was also employed at Llandygai (in a small stone circle outside the henge's entrance) and at the small stone circle of Balbirnie in Fife, Scotland.

This incorporation of the remains of the dead within stone circles such as Balbirnie and Stonehenge continued a relationship between megaliths and the dead that stretched back almost 1000 years in Britain and nearly 2000 years within Atlantic Europe. Archaeologists have long recognised this as evidence of ancestor-venerating practices amongst these early farmers, for whom genealogies were a means of creating kin groups large enough to work together in growing their food. By constructing the places of the ancestors in permanent materials – stone, earth and chalk – they were demonstrating the eternal presence of these ancestors in the transient world of the living. This eternal presence was further reinforced by linking certain monuments to the endless

Stonehenge for the ancestors

In 1998 Mike Parker Pearson invited his Malagasy colleague, Ramilisonina, to visit Stonehenge and Avebury. They had worked together for many years on the archaeology of Madagascar, where standing stones and stone monuments are still built today for the dead. Ramilisonina's own family put up megaliths so it was interesting to see what he made of Stonehenge. Ramilisonina could not believe that archaeologists had been unable to work out what it was for. In Madagascar, he explained, people build in stone for the ancestors because stone, like the ancestors, is eternal. Buildings for the living are made of wood because it, like human lives, is transient. Stonehenge was clearly a place of the ancestors.

Ramilisonina's idea echoed what several archaeologists were already thinking, and these theories were the impetus for a major project, the Stonehenge Riverside Project (see Chapter 5). The findings of this project confirmed Ramilisonina's predictions that Stonehenge was for the dead by recovering and dating its cremated human remains. The project also discovered an entirely unsuspected village – a place of the living – beneath the henge of Durrington Walls. It revealed the likely significance of the River Avon, linking Stonehenge and Durrington Walls via two ceremonial avenues. Stonehenge was thus one part of a much larger complex that stretched for 2 miles (3.2km) along the river.

Ethnographic analogy – making comparisons between the past and the present, and between one culture and another – is only one small part of archaeological reasoning. In this case, it helped provide a starting point for research: a set of predictions that could be compared with what actually lay under the ground. If the predictions had been wrong, then the idea could have been rejected. The theory that Stonehenge was associated with ancestors provided a short-cut to understanding that Stonehenge was part of a long tradition in Neolithic western European megalith-building from 4700 BC to 2000 BC: stone and earthen monuments were built for the dead and the ancestors, whilst Neolithic houses were built of perishable materials (except in treeless environments such as Orkney).

Figure 3.6 *Ramilisonina, the archaeologist from Madagascar whose ideas inspired the Stonehenge Riverside Project*

cycle of the heavens, notably the movements of the sun and the moon, through orientations and alignments towards key moments such as solstice sunrise and sunset.

The most dramatic feature of Stonehenge stage 1 is the presence of some 56 bluestones arranged as a stone circle within its Aubrey Holes, and another 25 or so such stones set up in a circle at the site known as Bluestonehenge beside the river at West Amesbury, a mile south-east of Stonehenge. To bring 80 or so bluestone pillars, each weighing 1–2 tons, from Wales, 140 miles (225km) away, must have been an extraordinary achievement requiring a significant level of co-operation between several territories. Opinion is divided about whether the bluestones were brought by sea or over land but, whichever way they came, their transport would have required lengthy negotiation between different territorial groups, long-term centralised planning, and complex organisation.

People had been exchanging polished axes of stone and flint over long distances across Britain for a thousand years before the bluestones were moved, so there were certainly long-distance routeways already in existence. Numerous 'axe factories' – where the axes were quarried and shaped – have been identified, so we know where many of them originated. The distinctive geology of one type of polished axe pinpoints its place of origin to the Preseli mountains in west Wales although its precise source has not yet been located. It is a different rock type to the Stonehenge bluestones but the products of this axe quarry are distributed throughout the valleys of south Wales, indicating the existence of inland routes leading eastwards from Preseli long before the bluestones were transported.

Similar cases of the long-distance movement of large stones are well documented for ancient Egypt, the Inca and the Roman Empire – all early state societies with stratified social classes of administrators and labourers, writing systems, tax collection and centralised bureaucracy. Neolithic societies in Britain (and the whole of Europe) were not that organised, and while social inequality was already in place, it would be 3000 years before the earliest state society in Britain. So how was the long-distance movement of bluestones possible?

To answer this question, we need to look at evidence for co-operative, communal and large-scale activities in this period. As described earlier, among the changes during the Middle Neolithic was the architectural innovation of the cursus, a type of monument that was not only indigenous in inspiration but was also constructed across almost the whole of Britain – far

Figure 3.7 (facing page) The towering sarsen trilithons dwarf the bluestones

more widely than previous monument types such as causewayed enclosures. Cursuses were built in Scotland, England and Wales and there may even be one at Newgrange in Ireland. In the same period, people across the whole of southern Britain adopted a new style of decorated pottery, known as Peterborough Ware; previously, in the Early Neolithic, different styles of pottery were used in different regions of southern England and Wales.

These changes at the monumental and domestic levels indicate a growing degree of commonality in people's use of material culture. Although there was no centralised state, no nationwide system of control, people seem to have belonged to a single culture, using the same objects and building the same monuments, with territorial boundaries not marked by changes in lifestyle or belief. While there was growing inequality *within* communities, there was also a wider sense of shared identity *between* communities.

Such changes were probably also occurring in Ireland. Archaeologists have worked out that the building materials for the Newgrange and Knowth tombs – quartz, granodiorite, granite cobbles, gabbro, siltstone cobbles, and greywacke and sandstone kerbstones – came from a wide hinterland stretching almost 100 miles (160km) along the east coast of Ireland. Perhaps what was important was not simply building these huge tombs but also incorporating material elements of different territories into these centralised places. Thus the tombs would have been the embodiment of many places in one.

The kerbstones used at Newgrange and Knowth each weigh about half a ton and number over 200. They were brought at least 3 miles (4.8km) from the coast in what must have been an epic feat of labour mobilisation. Just 240 miles (385km) or three days' sail across the Irish Sea from Pembrokeshire, tales of building the Boyne tombs might have reached the ears of people in west Wales and perhaps inspired them to move 80 bluestones an even greater distance.

Yet what was so special about the bluestones and, indeed, about the site of Stonehenge that they should be moved there, and nowhere else? There has been a lot of speculation about this question. Did Neolithic people think that the bluestones had healing properties, as claimed in Geoffrey of Monmouth's story? Or was it the acoustic properties of the bluestones that made them special – some of them make a slight ringing sound when struck. Neither of these ideas is convincing. The proponents of the healing theory point to the existence of folk-tales about holy wells

and healing springs on the south side of the Preseli mountains, but this doesn't help explain the movement of the bluestones, for which the recently identified sources are on the north side of the mountains, not near the medieval 'holy wells'. The 'ringing' theory about acoustics applies only to one sort of bluestone – the spotted dolerites – and ignores the other types of Welsh rocks present at Stonehenge such as rhyolites, sandstones and tuff.

A very convincing answer to why the bluestones were sought out was first articulated in 1956, when the great prehistorian Gordon Childe wrote that the movement of the bluestones must indicate 'a degree of political unification or a sacred peace'. Writing before the widespread application of radiocarbon-dating, Childe had no way of knowing the sequence of events and changes that are described above – he didn't know that the bluestones were moved during a time of growing commonality of material culture *c* 3000 BC. In spite of his lack of precise knowledge about the Middle and Late Neolithic, Childe had still hit upon the significant point about unification across a large territory.

Figure 3.8
Reconstruction drawing of Peterborough Ware vessels (© Chris Jones)

Figure 3.9 *An atmospheric view of Pentre Ifan dolmen in Pembrokeshire*

Pembrokeshire was a remarkable place in prehistory. Thriving populations of Mesolithic hunter-gatherers lived there from 10,000 years ago. With the beginning of the Neolithic, Pembrokeshire produced one of the densest concentrations of megalithic tombs in Britain. By 3700 BC, Early Neolithic people in the region were adept at lifting large capstones onto uprights to form dolmens (also known as cromlechs) for their dead. One of these capstones at the dolmen of Garn Turne weighs *c* 60 tons and seems to have been just a step too far for the Neolithic engineers, since it collapsed the chamber.

West Wales was also rather different from southern England in the Early Neolithic, having more in common with Ireland where we find similar tomb styles and material culture. Archaeologists have for a long time known that the Neolithic of western Britain was distinct from that of the south and east. The reason for this cultural difference in the Early Neolithic is uncertain but it may be due to the directions from which the farming way of life arrived in Britain, probably arriving separately in these two regions. This theory suggests that early farming in Wales and Ireland arrived via Brittany whereas farming was introduced into south-east England from northern France. Thus Neolithic people in Wales might have considered themselves to have had very different ancestries to those in southern England.

To elaborate on Childe's theory about bluestones and political unification, bringing the Welsh stones to the site of Stonehenge was perhaps an act that merged two different ancestries from two of the most ancient parts of Britain. Just why the precise location of Stonehenge was so important as an *axis mundi* has already been discussed in the last chapter. Effectively, two special and ancient places of origin were combined into one, unifying the east and west regions of southern Britain. Strontium isotope analysis (see p 88) of the teeth of two cows buried in the ditch at Stonehenge shows that one of them was raised in western Britain, far from the chalklands of Salisbury Plain; it could well have come from Pembrokeshire. Christopher Snoeck, a researcher at Oxford University, has discovered that some of the people whose cremated remains were buried at Stonehenge also came from western Britain.

Recent excavations at the places from which the bluestone

Figure 3.10 *The Preseli mountains in Pembrokeshire, seen from the east (© Sidney Howells)*

Carn Meini

Carn Breseb

Carn Gyfrwy

Carn Goedog

Carn Alw

came, on the northern slopes of the Preseli mountains, are adding new evidence to Childe's theory of unification. Geologists have identified three quarries by chemical and petrographic matching of bluestones from Stonehenge with specific rock outcrops in Pembrokeshire. The most common type of bluestone at Stonehenge is called spotted dolerite and this has been matched chemically to two outcrops on the north side of the Preseli mountains. One of these, Carn Goedog, has produced a number of matches, indicating that this is probably where most of Stonehenge's bluestones were obtained (see Fig 4.9). A second source of spotted dolerite bluestones is the smaller outcrop of Cerrigmarchogion, further west along the north side of the mountains. A third source is of rhyolite bluestone, pinned down to the outcrop of Craig Rhos-y-felin beside a small stream that flows down from its headwaters at Carn Goedog and Cerrigmarchogion. Geologists have been able to identify the precise spot on the Craig Rhos-y-felin rhyolite outcrop where an exact match can be found with samples of bluestone found at Stonehenge.

Figure 3.11 *The rock outcrop at Craig Rhos-y-felin, Pembrokeshire, where one of the bluestones was quarried. An abandoned pillar can be seen in the centre of the excavation*

Stonehenge and society

Archaeological excavations at Craig Rhos-y-felin have now revealed the recess in the rock face from which a rhyolite bluestone pillar was removed and taken to Stonehenge. Finds include hammerstones and worked flints. Radiocarbon dates indicate that the quarrying of megaliths took place at Craig Rhos-y-felin c 3400–3300 BC and later on in the Bronze Age after 2000 BC. Intriguingly, the quarrying activity took place directly on top of a sequence of hearths that date back much further – to just before 8000 BC. It is not impossible that this outcrop had a special significance long before farming arrived in Wales. The same may be the case for Carn Goedog, visited by Mesolithic hunters long before its dolerite pillars were quarried c 3300–3200 BC.

The bluestones were not put up at Stonehenge until c 2900 BC, and our date for the quarrying in Wales is c 3300 BC. It seems unlikely that the journey could have taken 400 years; what is more plausible is that the quarried bluestones were originally set up as one or more stone monuments in Pembrokeshire. Perhaps the original motivation for the quarrying was to build a tomb such as a passage grave. The Stonehenge bluestones are of various types that can be obtained within a small area within this part of Wales, so perhaps local Neolithic people were interested in finding enough of them within a suitably short distance of where they wanted to build their monuments. If this was the case, the precise type of rock was not important, merely the distance to the outcrops where such pillars could be found.

If the quarries were intended to supply local monuments then we can start the search for these potential local stone tombs by looking not very far away from the sources of the rocks. The stream along which the known rock sources lie flows through a steep-sided valley that has only a few points of access. This difficult topography would have limited the directions in which the detached bluestone pillars could have been taken when they left the quarry. One of these points of access to the valley leads to the Iron Age hillfort of Castell Mawr, a site suspected as having been originally a Neolithic henge before being re-used in the Iron Age 2000 years later. Excavations at Castell Mawr in 2013 did indeed reveal a hole for a since-vanished standing stone but radiocarbon dating demonstrated that the stone was either put up or taken down in the Bronze Age, too late for it to have been taken to Stonehenge. Nearly a mile south of Castell Mawr is another access point where it is easy to walk out of the valley. Geophysical survey here has revealed what may be an undiscovered Middle Neolithic 'passage grave' tomb. Future

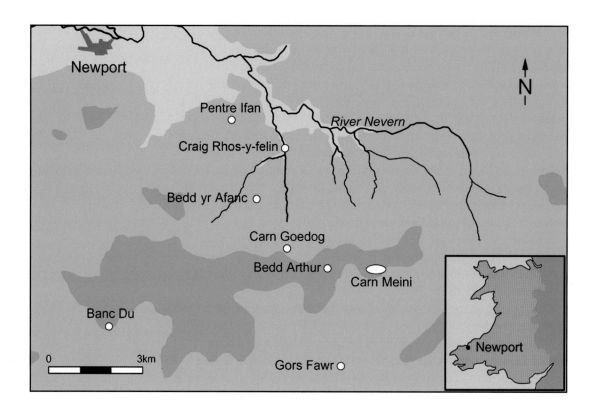

Figure 3.12 *Map showing the locations of Carn Goedog, Craig Rhos-y-felin and other prehistoric sites in the Preseli mountains (© Irene de Luis)*

excavation will reveal whether this is a location at which the bluestones were originally erected.

It is also possible that some or all of the bluestones were taken directly to Salisbury Plain from their quarries in Preseli. The dates from Craig Rhos-y-felin are the same as the dates of long barrows on Salisbury Plain, and a broken pillar of spotted dolerite was found in one of these barrows. This is Boles Barrow, excavated in 1801 by William Cunnington, who noted, among the locally derived sarsens covering the burials in the tomb, a 'Blue hard Stone also, ye same to some of the upright Stones in ye inner Circle at Stonehenge.' Boles Barrow lies 12 miles (19km) west of Stonehenge, so this stone may have been deposited in the barrow *en route* to the Stonehenge area.

The Boles Barrow stone may be evidence that any bluestone predecessor monument in Preseli was short-lived, if such a structure was ever built at all, and it also points to a 500-year presence of the bluestones on Salisbury Plain before they were erected at Stonehenge *c* 2900 BC. Just where they might have stood during that time is unknown; perhaps they formed one or more stone circles or even adorned some of the region's long barrows.

Meanings of stone monuments around the world

Many traditional societies build megalithic monuments, or used to build them in recent centuries. In Madagascar, in Indonesia (on the island of Sumba and elsewhere), in Vanuatu in the South Pacific, and amongst the Naga of India there are well-documented traditions of megalith-building, in all cases for the ancestors. Ancient African megalithic sites in Senegal and Ethiopia have been found on excavation to be places of burial. Even the British and European historical tradition of erecting gravestones as permanent markers of the dead is an example of this association of stone with the memory and presence of the ancestral dead.

In traditional societies where people erect megalithic monuments today, it is rare that such monuments are *not* for the dead and the ancestors. The supposedly mysterious statues of Rapa Nui (Easter Island) were described by the islanders as being images of their ancestors. The earliest written evidence of an association between stone and the dead comes from an inscription on an 8th-century BC standing stone in Turkey, which records that the soul of a man called Kuttamuwa is in that stone. In the 6th century BC, the Chinese sage Laozi wrote that 'the hard and the strong are the comrades of death, the supple and the weak are the comrades of life'.

While the association of stone with the permanence of the afterlife is not universal, it does crop up with considerable frequency. This is probably not something hard-wired into the human brain but rather a useful metaphor for thinking about life and death. People in many different parts of the world, at many different times, have drawn upon this metaphor to make sense of their world and to express their identity through tangible manifestations of the dead and the ancestors.

Figure 3.13 *A modern-day stone tomb in southern Madagascar. Note the two upright pillars on the edges of the tomb and the numerous cows' horns decorating the tomb's interior (© Mike Parker Pearson)*

Stonehenge stage 2 – a meeting house for the ancestors, c 2500 BC

The people who were buried at Stonehenge have left little evidence of who they were. Why did they merit such an important place of burial? Unlike earlier elite burials elsewhere in Britain, these burials do not have many grave goods to indicate a high station in life. One cremation burial was accompanied by a stone mace-head; a pottery disc may have accompanied another. While these are simple objects, they are rare and important. The mace appears to have been a symbol of authority in Neolithic and Bronze Age Britain, so at least one person buried at Stonehenge was provided with a high-status item. The pottery disc was burnt on one side and may have been an incense burner, which could signify religious duties; only one other similar disc is known, from the henge complex at Dorchester in Dorset.

Most of the cremated remains from Stonehenge are those of adult men and women. There are very few teenagers or children – just four individuals. This is far too low a number for a pre-modern population with high rates of child mortality. Thus there was a choice being made about who was buried here: preference was given to adults of both sexes, with most young people being buried elsewhere. Many of the people whose remains were buried at Stonehenge suffered from osteoarthritis in the lower back, indicative of a life of relatively hard physical labour. Only one individual showed evidence of disease – a cavity in the back of the knee caused by a widening of the artery. (This condition, known as a popliteal aneurysm, rarely has any symptoms but is eventually fatal without amputation or modern surgery.)

It is difficult to be absolutely sure that these people were drawn from a political or religious elite but this is the most likely conclusion. What is interesting is that their burials seem to be a secondary aspect of the monument. The monument does not seem to have been built to 'house' those buried there, in contrast to what was probably the case at Knowth and Newgrange in Ireland. Overall, elites do not reveal themselves with any clarity in the archaeological record of the early 3rd millennium BC. Archaeologists have to look hard to find them since the

Figure 3.14
The polished stone mace-head found in a cremation burial at Stonehenge. This is one of only a very few grave goods recovered from the site. As with other mace-heads, such as that from Knowth (see Fig 3.5), the stone appears to have been selected and polished to accentuate the patterns in the stone (© The Salisbury Museum)

Stonehenge and society

burial rites of cremation at that time seem to present a picture
of relative equality. Of course, this does not mean that people
were actually equal in life. One aspect of life where the otherwise
hidden social structure is revealed is in the domestic architecture
at Durrington Walls. Houses there did not vary much in size;
there are no palaces, since most of the buildings are about 5.3 x
5.3m in floor size. The only variation in size is between private
houses and public monuments, with the latter being many times
larger. However, there are clues about social inequalities between
households according to their use, position and internal design.

Within the east entrance of the Durrington Walls settlement,
one of the houses was divided off from the others by a wooden
fence. Not only did it have its own outhouse but both structures
had their walls covered with cobb (a bright white cement of chalk
lumps) rather than simply clay daub as found on the walls of the

Figure 3.15
*One of the high-
status houses under
excavation within the
centre of Durrington
Walls. A line of
postholes from an
encircling fence is
clearly visible at top
left*

other houses. In addition, this house had relatively little pottery on its midden (rubbish heap), perhaps indicating that the people who lived in this house did not do their own cooking: the lack of broken cooking pots suggests that their food must have come from another building. This is corroborated by the wood burned on the houses' hearths. Specialists in plant remains can identify tree species from ancient charcoal, and there was relatively little oak charcoal from this house, in contrast to the others; oak burns slowly and steadily and is an excellent fuel for cooking.

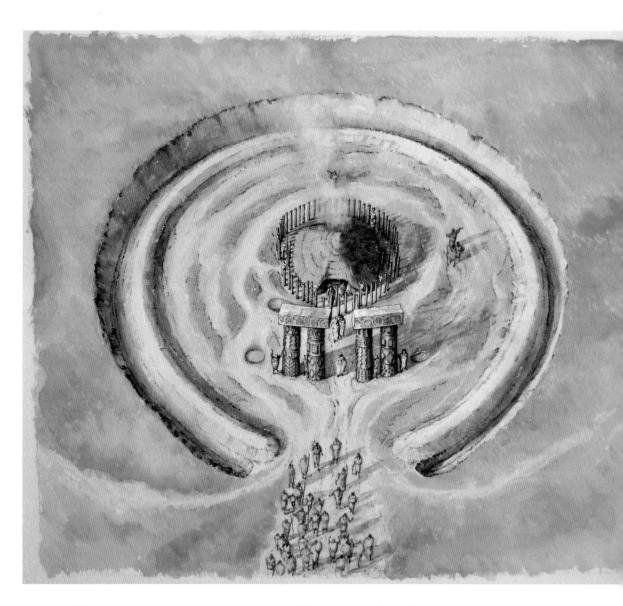

Stonehenge and society

Near the centre of Durrington Walls there is a series of five small circular enclosures; two of them have been investigated and found to contain remains of houses. The central one was probably that of a leading family or household, perhaps those overseeing the building of Stonehenge stage 2 (the stone circle and trilithons). Although this house is the same size as the others, it sits within its own enclosure, 40m in diameter, and was surrounded by a circular palisade of timber posts; it was entered by walking between large posts flanking the approach. The entire enclosure was much cleaner than other areas of settlement at Durrington Walls, indicating that this building might have had more than ordinary significance, as well as being the residence of someone very important. Inside the house, the roof was supported on four posts which would have given it a much more impressive appearance than the other houses, which had simple pitched roofs supported only by the walls. The central position of this house provided views of the entire settlement, especially towards the Southern Circle and the avenue leading down to the river.

The fact that those of higher social status chose not to live in larger houses than the rest of the community, and that burial rites broadly reinforced this notion of equality in material things, tells us something very interesting about leadership in the society that built Stonehenge. This was no pharaoh-led society in which rulers were treated as semi-divine individuals. There must have been leaders to organise such a major feat of engineering, transport and logistics, but archaeologically they appear to have been much the same as everyone else, apart perhaps from some differences in their houses which may reflect their high status. Whether the leaders were elected or chosen on ability rather than acquiring power by birth and genealogy we cannot say.

The circular arrangement of the Durrington Walls settlement also suggests an attempt at organising the different groups living there into a non-hierarchical order. Circles have no top or bottom, no head or sides. Circles can disguise leadership and power. The round-robin letter employed by sailors and pirates ensured that no ringleaders of a complaint could be identified since everyone signed on a circular list of signatures. Thus the circular arrangement of the Durrington Walls village perhaps gave no superiority to any one group over another except for those living within the five central enclosures. Thus it seems the society that built Stonehenge was indeed a hierarchical one but its leaders played down visible, tangible expressions of their authority.

Figure 3.16
(facing page) A reconstruction by Peter Dunn of the prestige house in its enclosure at the centre of Durrington Walls. The house, which was of a different construction to the others in the settlement, was approached through large flanking timber posts (© Peter Dunn)

Figure 3.17 *A reconstruction of how the settlement at Durrington Walls might have looked at its height. Hundreds of houses form a ring on the line of the later henge, while an avenue runs down to the banks of the Avon (© Peter Dunn)*

Community values were emphasised over personal authority in order to complete this massive undertaking successfully.

Archaeologists have wondered just how far people travelled to take part in building Stonehenge. Isotope analysis can help us answer this question, but as there are only a few human remains surviving from *c* 2500 BC in the Stonehenge area, it is difficult to be sure where people came from. There is, however, a single stray tooth from Durrington Walls which belonged to someone who was definitely not local – analysis shows they grew up in western Britain, either Wales or north Devon. More useful information can be obtained from the teeth of cattle and pigs; there are tens of thousands of animal bones from Durrington Walls, the remains of great feasts. Only a small proportion of the cows came from the chalklands around Stonehenge: the remainder came from at least 20 to 30 miles (30–45km) away and, indeed, some of these animals were raised on geology that is found only in highland Scotland, 400 miles (650km) to the north. Similar results are being obtained from analysis of the pig teeth.

Isotope analysis

Analysis of chemical isotopes is a new technique for establishing whether ancient people and their animals grew up in regions distant to where they ended up. Our bones and teeth absorb minerals from the food we eat and the water we drink. In the case of our teeth, these are absorbed into the enamel in childhood and do not change during adult life. Our bones, on the other hand, continue to absorb chemical elements until we die. Analysis of strontium isotopes in an adult's tooth enamel thus reveals the type of geology of the area where that person grew up. The chalk of southern England has a low isotopic value whereas the gneiss and granite of highland Scotland have a high value.

Oxygen isotope analysis of tooth enamel allows archaeological scientists to work out whether individuals grew up in cold and inland regions of Europe such as the Alps, or in warm and maritime environments such as western Britain.

The Beaker People Project has examined human bones from the time of stages 3–5 at Stonehenge (2400–1500 BC), using these methods to establish the lifetime mobility (since childhood) of 264 individuals. This period, the Copper Age and Early Bronze Age, was a time when new customs and new technology arrived from Europe. A third of these people were buried in places different to those where they grew up, but while some individuals, such as the Amesbury Archer, had migrated from mainland Europe, the majority of people were mobile only within Britain.

Analysis of different growth rings in individual cattle teeth shows that they came to Durrington Walls in a journey of a single stage, rather than in fits and starts. This is consistent with the cattle having been brought from their owners' home territory direct to Salisbury Plain rather than being traded down the line from distant places. We can reasonably use the cattle and pigs as a proxy for their human owners, who brought their living larders with them on the way to Stonehenge.

The long-distance involvement of people and animals from as far away as Scotland and western Britain shows that Stonehenge's 'catchment' was island-wide. This was an area far bigger than would have been needed if Stonehenge was built with efficiency as an important factor. An efficient use of resources would have sourced all that was technically essential from no further away than was necessary. This involvement of distant regions tells us that people from all over Britain wanted to be involved, in a widespread expression of group identity and unity.

The architecture of Stonehenge and the Durrington timber circles also provides us with insights into how this identity was expressed in material form. Both Woodhenge and Durrington Walls' Southern Circle consisted of six concentric rings of wooden posts, whilst the Northern Circle had only a single ring. Yet none of them seems to have been roofed. The Southern Circle was clearly open to the elements since there was no sign of an indoor floor surface or a surrounding eaves-drip gully (where rainwater erodes a small gully around a building as it drips persistently off a roof). These timber circles were public structures within which large numbers of people could gather beneath the open sky.

One structure that was roofed was a building with a D-shaped plan, 11m x 13m across, that lay immediately north of the Southern Circle. During excavation in 1967 it was found to have filled up with rubbish and was therefore initially interpreted as a midden. However, it was originally a building with a chalk plaster floor and surrounding stake-holes for the walls, just like other buildings at Durrington Walls. The absence of a hearth in this D-shaped building suggests that this was some sort of public building, not a house. Pots that contained milk were placed here and at the entrance to the Southern Circle, perhaps as offerings.

The building's D-plan made it a perfect gathering space, rather like a cinema or a lecture theatre. Other such D-plan structures have been found at Stonehenge itself, positioned just within the south entrance into the enclosure, and at Avebury, but the most famous example is the horseshoe arrangement of the five

Figure 3.18 *The Neolithic village of Skara Brae in Orkney, dating from c 3200 BC*

trilithons within the centre of Stonehenge. Effectively, Stonehenge was a stone version of meeting-houses that were normally built of wood, an eternal place of council for the varied ancestors of the people of Britain.

During the 500 years before Stonehenge stage 2 (the sarsen circle and trilithons) was built *c* 2500 BC, the people of Britain had developed increasingly similar tastes, acquiring a single identity in terms of material expression. By 2900 BC a single style of pottery – Grooved Ware – was in use all over Britain, replacing all previous regional forms. Grooved Ware originated in Orkney, in the far north, and spread south through the whole island. Classic henges, also apparently originating in Orkney, were also taken up across the length and breadth of the land. Even the styles of houses built at Durrington Walls were of a uniform type that was in use in Wales, Scotland, the Midlands and northern England, and Ireland. Once again, this architectural form appears to have evolved in Orkney, *c* 3200 BC. At Skara Brae these houses survive in their entirety, furniture and all: Neolithic Orcadians had cleared their forests by this date and had to build everything in stone, whether for the living or the dead.

Skara Brae was built *c* 3200 BC but the last phase of that site dates to around the time of Durrington Walls. The interior plans of some of the houses at these two sites are so similar that they can be overlaid without there being very much difference in size, shape, or arrangement of furniture. Interestingly, the Skara Brae houses share the same spatial hierarchy as found among the houses at Durrington Walls' east entrance. One house and its outhouse are separated from the others, not by a fence as at Durrington Walls but by a long passageway. Perhaps this model of a main house with a storage building and dependent houses was shared widely across Britain at that time.

Since Britain had become unified in its material culture and overall lifestyle, it may seem hard to understand why an island-wide demonstration of shared ancestral identity – the building of Stonehenge – might be needed. What was the chain of events that galvanized communities across the whole of Britain to erect the greatest stone monument of European prehistory? An answer may lie in Britain's changing relationship with Europe. During the first half of the 3rd millennium BC, the people of southern Britain seem not to have engaged in any visible trade or exchange with the Continent. As far as we can tell, no trade items crossed the Channel and no styles of ceramics or other artefacts were transferred from one side to the other.

All this changed in the middle of the millennium with the arrival of the Bell Beaker 'package' – metallurgy, the wheel and distinctive new burial rites and styles of dress all arrived from Europe. The complete Bell Beaker way of life – and way of death – did not take off in Britain until *c* 2450–2400 BC, a century after Stonehenge stage 2 was built, so can this new culture's arrival, which affected British society so profoundly, have caused Stonehenge to be built?

An answer may come from the discovery of a sherd of Bell Beaker pottery on the floor of one of the houses at Durrington Walls. This tallies with an earlier find of supposed Bell Beaker sherds below the henge bank in 1917. So perhaps Bell Beaker pottery was actually in use in Britain as early as 2500 BC, indicating that Britain's long period of isolation had ended and people were crossing the Channel, bringing new lifestyles, languages, dress and religion. Within a hundred years, incomers and natives were adopting the burial rites that the immigrants had brought from their homelands.

Bell Beaker-using people were expert metallurgists and one reason for migrating to Britain was the availability of ores of copper and gold in this island. The spread of the 'Beaker folk' was also an endless search for land across western Europe, where they colonised new spaces as well as sharing territories with indigenous groups. This colonising process was achieved not in horde-like invasions sweeping into new territories and conquering all before them, but in short-distance movements and hops by individuals and small groups. Of course, the level of organisation necessary to cross the Channel might have necessitated coming in larger numbers but even so it was not an all-out invasion – more a long-running flow of immigrants over many centuries.

Some archaeologists have wondered whether these immigrants were drawn to Britain because of Stonehenge, that perhaps this was a place of pilgrimage. The Amesbury Archer, for example, buried 3 miles (4.8km) away, came from somewhere

Figure 3.19 *A Long-Necked Beaker from Winterbourne Stoke G54 bowl barrow, excavated by the 18th-century antiquarian William Cunnington (height: 150mm) (© Wiltshire Museum, Devizes)*

Stonehenge and society

in the middle of Europe (see Fig 1.25). However, when viewed in the context of the hundreds of Bell Beaker burials from across Britain, Stonehenge and Salisbury Plain were no more special attractions than other regions such as the Peak District and East Yorkshire. In fact, the majority of the long-distance Bell Beaker migrants to the Stonehenge area had grown up most probably in western Britain; many of the people buried here in the Beaker fashion were not locals but neither were they European immigrants.

Stonehenge stages 3–4 – minor modifications to the monument

After the main stage of building Stonehenge *c* 2500 BC, its stones were reorganised on only two further occasions, *c* 2400 BC (stage 3) when the Stonehenge Avenue was built, and *c* 2100 BC (stage 4). The first of these rearrangements of stones – a bluestone circle thought to be the relocated stones from Bluestonehenge – happened not long before a large hole was dug against the base of the great trilithon. The hole was later filled in and when, in stage 4, some bluestones were rearranged into an inner oval, inside the sarsen trilithon horseshoe, one of the bluestones was set into the top of the filled-in hole.

Why the hole was dug is a mystery but it was eventually responsible for toppling the great trilithon at an unknown later date. Was it an act of iconoclasm, carried out by a group attempting to desecrate the monument and what it stood for? The period *c* 2400 BC was the swansong of the megalith- and mound-building way of life that had lasted in Britain for over 1000 years. Amongst the earliest Bell Beaker users were emigrants from Continental societies that had long ago stopped building megaliths for the ancestors or labouring in large work gangs to construct great monuments. They came from socially and politically decentralised societies in mainland Europe where megalith-building had been discontinued *c* 2800 BC at the latest. As Bell Beaker identities became evermore widespread within Britain, so the traditional religious beliefs and labour obligations grew weaker.

Yet Stonehenge continued to be of religious importance to the people who built cemeteries of round barrows in its vicinity. Stonehenge stage 4 (the final rearrangement of bluestones) coincided with a new fashion for large and elaborate round

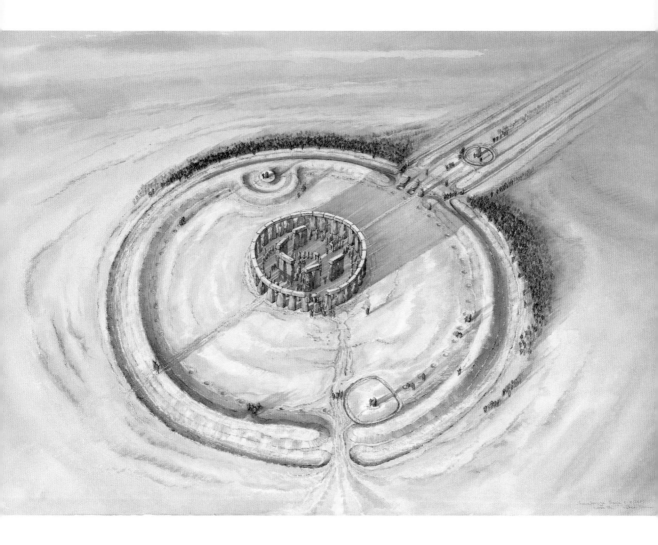

Figure 3.20
Stonehenge as it would have looked in stage 3, when the Avenue was constructed to the north-east (© Peter Dunn)

barrows. The individual dead of a particular lineage, rather than distant collective ancestors, were now most people's concern. Stonehenge provided a backdrop, redolent of authority from the deep ancestral past, for those families laying claim with their barrows to the land around it.

Ultimately, the new ways made Stonehenge increasingly obsolete. Even a show of rebuilding the great stone circle *c* 2100 BC (stage 4) could not alter these new circumstances. The modifications within Stonehenge were slight, involving simply the rearranging of bluestones into a new circle around an inner oval. The workforce needed would not have been that large – no more than a few hundred probably – and might not have stood out particularly among the many other groups building large barrows in sight of Stonehenge at that time. Honouring the ancient ancestors at Stonehenge was being out-classed by the needs of the newly dead, many of whom were being buried with golden grave goods.

The final modification of Stonehenge (stage 5) *c* 1600 BC – the Y and Z holes – looks incomplete and unfinished. Construction at Stonehenge ended not with a bang but a whimper.

Building
Stonehenge

4

S tonehenge was the last great megalithic monument of
the Neolithic. The first monuments were built 6000 years
earlier in south-eastern Turkey, at a group of sites in the
Upper Euphrates river valley. The principal of these is Göbekli
Tepe, a sequence of buildings forming a 'tell' or settlement mound,
dating to *c* 9500–9000 BC. Each building incorporated a dozen or
more standing stones, carefully carved out of limestone brought
from nearby quarries. Animals and other motifs were carved on
these T-shaped standing stones, which are clearly representations
of human forms; arms and hands are outlined on some of them.
There is uncertainty about whether the buildings at Göbekli Tepe

Figure 4.1 *(facing
page) Re-erecting
a trilithon at
Stonehenge during
William Hawley's
excavations in the
1920s (Reproduced
by permission of
Historic England)*

Figure 4.2 *Carved
megaliths at the site
of Göbekli Tepe, in
south-east Turkey.
The stones, dated to
c 9500–9000 BC, are
some of the earliest
megaliths in the
world (© Mike Parker
Pearson)*

were used as domestic dwellings or were 'inhabited' solely by these silent stone beings. Were they deities, ancestors or living people, represented in stone? No one knows for certain but the current opinion is that these carved stones represent celebrated ancestors of dispersed communities which came together at the dawn of the Neolithic.

Europe's megaliths before Stonehenge

The next megaliths to be built were those of Brittany and perhaps Portugal, more than 4000 years later and over 2000 miles away from south-eastern Turkey. It is highly unlikely that there was any connection at all with Göbekli Tepe. The western Atlantic megalithic tradition almost certainly developed independently of this earlier appearance. Nearly a century ago, academics thought that particular phenomena such as megalith-building were passed down from an ancient 'master race' and spread throughout the world to lesser and more-primitive cultures in a process called hyper-diffusion. With improved knowledge of chronology it is clear that these early Near Eastern monuments had nothing at all to do with the Atlantic megaliths which, in turn, had no influence upon, for example, megalith-building in India or Korea during the first millennium BC or in modern-day Indonesia or Madagascar.

Yet there are certain themes that they have in common. The vast majority of megalith-building societies in the past and the present have reserved these structures for the dead and the ancestors. Göbekli Tepe and the Atlantic megaliths also share similar contexts within the process of adopting agriculture. The most persuasive theory about the reasons for building megaliths and earthen monuments is that, as farming spread into regions with low population densities, so people needed something to bring them together in large-enough numbers for sowing, weeding and harvesting. Building monumental versions of their domestic houses in stone and earth was a good way not only of mobilising the scattered population but also of reinforcing their kinship connections, through descent from shared ancestors, with ancestral ceremonies at these monuments.

The earliest megalithic monuments built in western Europe were the large stone tombs and standing stones of Brittany, dating to 4700–4000 BC. One of the largest tombs is Barnanez, built in stone in the form of a rectangular timber house but with, along one side, a row of eleven passages each leading to a circular stone

chamber for the dead. Amongst the most impressive monuments of this date in Brittany is Le Grand Menhir Brisé, a 20.3m-long megalith weighing about 280 tons and moved almost 4 miles (6.4km) from its place of origin. This stone is approximately seven times heavier than the largest of Stonehenge's stones and yet a group of early farmers in Brittany, using only stone tools and timber, were able to move it a reasonable distance. They almost managed to stand it erect but the task was too much and the menhir fell and broke.

Brittany is also home to the Neolithic stone rows of Carnac. Within the Carnac area there are more than a dozen multiple rows made up of over 3000 standing stones; the largest monuments are Ménec, Kermario, Kerlescan and Kerzerho. The Ménec monument consists of eleven rows of standing stones running for a distance of about ¾ mile (*c* 1 km). The Carnac rows are undated and it is possible that, whatever their Neolithic origins, they were gradually added to intermittently into the historical period. However, on what is now the off-shore island of Hoëdic, a smaller, single alignment of standing stones at Douet has been dated, to 4700–4500 BC. One of its standing stones is known as La Dame de Hoëdic, a stone with a natural shoulder on one side, natural 'breasts' and partially carved 'legs'. Archaeologist Chris Scarre interprets this and other Breton megaliths as deliberate resemblances of human forms – the spirits of the dead in stone.

Figure 4.3 *Le Grand Menhir Brisé, Carnac, France. This stone, which is over 20m in length, is the largest menhir (standing stone) in the world. Now broken into four pieces, the stone weighed c 280 tons. Like the stones at Stonehenge, it was transported over several kilometres to its present location (© Chris Scarre)*

Figure 4.4 *The stone rows at Kermario, Carnac (© Chris Scarre)*

A massive feat of megalith-building produced the Cueva de Menga at Antequera in southern Spain, *c* 2500 BC. This is the largest megalithic tomb in Europe, constructed with enormous stone slabs, the heaviest of which is one of the capstones which weighs 250 tons. A workforce of thousands must have been required to build this enormous edifice.

Engineering feats of lesser renown were commonplace across Atlantic Europe during the first few thousand years of farming. There are more than 10,000 Neolithic megalithic monuments surviving in Western Europe, from Sweden to southern Spain. The vast majority are relatively small-scale and would have required only moderate and local levels of community participation. In all these cases nobody felt any need to go that extra mile and construct a 'super-monument' like Newgrange, Avebury or Stonehenge.

The Early Neolithic tombs of Britain and Ireland are, by and large, small-scale monuments built by small workforces. Yet something changed, first in Ireland and then Britain, after *c* 3200 BC, during the Middle Neolithic. Much wider community involvement was now possible in a way that never happened in the megalith-building societies in Scandinavia, Germany, the Netherlands or France in this period after 4000 BC. Part of the reason for this was the rise of social inequality in Britain and Ireland, perhaps affected by these islands' increased isolation from the rest of Europe, but another aspect must have been the rise of religious ideologies powerful enough to inspire thousands to work at the direction of a few.

Special places and natural wonders

It is not possible to get a very clear picture of the religious motivations behind these Irish and British mega-monuments but an emerging line of evidence is the significance of *place*, which seems to have been rather different to the use of landscape on the Continent. In the British Isles, certain locations appear to have gathered long 'histories' of use and significance, often incorporating natural features into their very fabric. As we have seen in Chapter 2, Stonehenge is an excellent example of this, perhaps the paramount example, but other cases are emerging elsewhere in Britain. In Orkney, a large settlement has been discovered at the Ness of Brodgar, on a narrow peninsula which has the Stones of Stenness at one end and the Ring of Brodgar at the other. The orientation of this peninsula is towards midwinter solstice sunrise in one direction and midsummer sunset in the other. The settlement on the Ness is also located so as to have a clear view of the midwinter solstice sun setting in a notch between two mountains on the neighbouring island of Hoy.

A similar link between land and heavens has been suggested for the stone circle of Calanais on the Isle of Lewis in the Outer Hebrides, except in this case the link is to the movement of the moon. Every 18.6 years the moon appears to skim along the horizon to the south, the direction in which there is a natural stone outcrop, Cnoc An Tursa, that looks uncannily like a Neolithic megalithic tomb.

At Avebury, the special dimension of its place might have been, in part, the inter-relationship between land and water, as springs and intermittent seasonal streams changed the valley bottom here from dry to wet and back again. It is also a landscape that was marked by often dense spreads of sarsen stone, affording it a physical quality distinct from other areas of southern England.

Such special places were perhaps seen as natural wonders or *axes mundi* where earth and heaven coincided and the mysteries

Figure 4.5 *The recently excavated settlement at the Ness of Brodgar in Orkney. The Stones of Stenness can be seen across the water*

of the universe might be revealed. Thus they provided another sense of place that went beyond the local and the ordinary. Every now and again people came in large numbers from far and near to re-make such places. Avebury, for example, went through at least four stages of construction involving the erection of *c* 500 standing stones, some of them weighing up to 100 tons.

Building megalithic monuments

As we have seen in Chapter 2, Stonehenge was the most complex of all these super-monuments, requiring enormous levels of long-distance co-operation in the first two of its five stages of construction.

To build a megalithic monument requires considerable resources. A large labour force is only one element of a complex and lengthy process of planning and resourcing. Years before the start of the actual building project, alliances and agreements must be put in place. People also need to gather the raw materials to make rope, build scaffolding and dig holes. This means enormous quantities of timber, antler pick-axes and whatever was used for rope-making. Lime bast (from beneath the tree bark) and cattle hides have been suggested as suitable materials but an actual prehistoric rope, used for pulling a large timber, has been found in position at the site of Seahenge in Norfolk. The rope was made of twisted strands of honeysuckle and the large timber to which it was attached has been dated by its tree rings to 2049 BC.

Every army marches on its stomach, and the huge food resources needed would have had to be planned years in advance. Pigs and cattle had to be raised in time to be eaten by the workers, along with wild and domestic plant foods. Ethnographic examples of megalith-moving in Madagascar and Indonesia show that no expense is spared in planning feasts for the participants. The evidence for such feasting at Durrington Walls is clear – huge quantities of pork and beef were consumed, with articulated animal bones indicating that half-eaten joints of meat were discarded on the middens rather than being stripped of every ounce of nutrition.

Figure 4.6 *(left) A cache of antler picks found at Durrington Walls. (© Mike Parker Pearson)*

Figure 4.7 *(right) The rope of twisted honeysuckle that was used to erect the tree trunk in the replica of Seahenge (© Francis Pryor)*

Stonehenge stage 1 – bringing stones from Wales

The actual construction of stage 1 at Stonehenge was not a huge undertaking – erecting the standing stones and digging the enclosure ditch were not massive tasks – it was getting the stones there that must have taken an extraordinary amount of effort, co-operation and planning.

To move 80 megalithic stones 180 miles (140 miles as the crow flies; 290km/225km) is a remarkable achievement for a society without wheels or modern machinery. Even though recent laser-scanning of the bluestones at Stonehenge has revealed that most of them weigh between 1 and 2 tons each (rather than the 4 tons once estimated), this was still a very tricky undertaking.

Until geologists identified the source of the Stonehenge bluestones as being on the north side of the Preseli mountains and further north in the Nevern valley, there had been a general assumption that the stones were dragged off the south side of the hills and taken to the deep natural harbour at Milford Haven, whence they were rafted along the Welsh coast to the area of Avonmouth. From there, rafts could have travelled along the Bristol Avon before the stones were landed and dragged the rest of the way onto Salisbury Plain. This hypothetical route is now thought to be unlikely because the stones came from the north side of the Preselis. The Milford Haven route idea took another knock when geologists discovered that the 5m-long Altar Stone is not from the Cosheston beds of Milford Haven as once thought, but from another sandstone source altogether, possibly in the Brecon Beacons and certainly nowhere near Milford Haven or the coast.

Thanks to the new geological research, it is now clear that the bluestones can only have been taken one of two ways: either by sea from the mouth of the River Nevern to the Bristol Avon; or overland along river valleys running from Crymych to Carmarthen to Brecon to Usk, and then by raft across the River Severn and along the Bristol Avon. The nautical route is an attractive one. It appeals to our imagination and, at first sight, it seems the easiest way to move large stones, although many years ago archaeologist Richard Atkinson pointed out that the passage around Pembrokeshire's western peninsula is very dangerous because of its steep cliffs, submerged rocks, tidal races, whirlpools and eddies.

Building Stonehenge

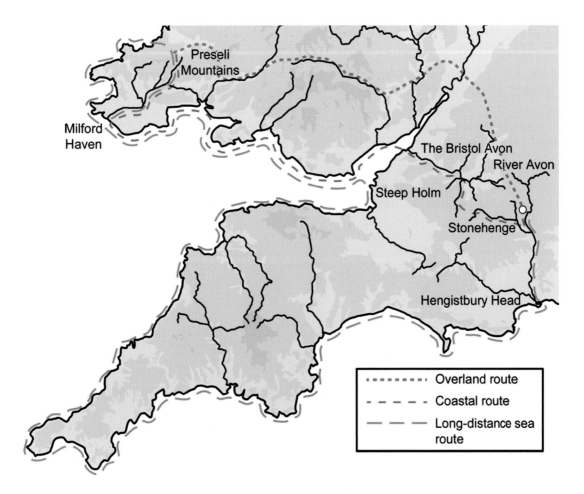

Figure 4.8 *Map showing the possible routes for transporting the bluestones from west Wales (© Irene de Luis)*

It is only recently that the land route has been considered a possible valid alternative. Yet valleys were useful routeways in prehistory, colonised from at least the Neolithic onwards, so long-established paths probably preceded modern roads such as the A40 that runs along most of this route through Brecon to Usk. The uneven ground need not have been a major obstacle – ethnographic evidence from early 20th-century Assam in India shows that a megalith of bluestone-size can be carried on interwoven lattices of wooden poles by 40 or so men across difficult terrain.

The 'land route', of course, still entailed crossing water: the River Severn would have to be negotiated, with the stones on rafts or slung between boats, but at least these waters would be calm, in contrast to the sea route around the Welsh coast. If the Altar Stone did indeed come from the Brecon area then the land

Finding the sources of Stonehenge's bluestones

Ever since the 17th century, it has been thought that the sarsen stones had a local origin in Wessex. John Aubrey, appointed royal antiquary by Charles II, thought the Marlborough Downs, 20 miles (32km) north of Stonehenge, to be their most likely source, and some 60 years later, William Stukeley came to the same conclusion. It was not until 1923, however, that the geologist H H Thomas established that the bluestone pillars originated from outcrops in the Preseli mountains of Pembrokeshire, in west Wales.

In 2011 a major break-through was made by geologists Rob Ixer and Richard Bevins in identifying the exact source of the bluestones. While searching through the stores of Salisbury Museum, Mike Parker Pearson and Colin Richards had come across a

Figure 4.9 *Carn Goedog in the Preseli mountains, the principal source of the bluestones*

shoebox of bluestone chippings found in 1947 in a field half a mile (0.8km) north-west of Stonehenge. They passed these stones to the geologists who made an unexpected discovery: most of these chippings were of a type of rhyolite that they had also found in large quantities among debris from the 2008 excavations at Stonehenge. Bevins had been working on the geology of west Wales for decades and was puzzled by this unusual type of rhyolite: it contains a mineral called stilpnomelane and all his previous chemical analyses had shown that this mineral could not be found in the region.

In a 'eureka' moment Bevins remembered that, many years before, he had collected samples from an impressive rhyolite outcrop in Pembrokeshire but had never got around to analysing them. They came from Craig Rhos-y-felin, beside a tributary of the River Nevern off the northern edge of the Preseli mountains. When Bevins analysed these samples, he found that they were an exact chemical match for the chippings from Stonehenge. Ixer's petrographic microscope analysis of the rhyolite's structure revealed that it has a unique fabric, created by the way that this former sheet of lava had cooled and folded. Having taken samples along the outcrop at Craig Rhos-y-felin, Ixer and Bevins found that this fabric can be matched precisely at only one spot. As archaeological excavation later revealed, they had found the exact location where one of Stonehenge's bluestones was detached from the rock (see Fig 3.11).

In 2014, Bevins and Ixer carried out a chemical and statistical analysis of twelve of the spotted dolerite bluestones from Stonehenge and found that they can be matched with three sources in the Preseli mountains. The main one of these is the outcrop of Carn Goedog, at the top of the valley from Craig Rhos-y-felin. The second is Cerrigmarchogion, a little to the west of Carn Goedog, and the third is in the vicinity of these, quite possibly also Carn Goedog. Their discovery revealed that archaeologists looking for the source of the bluestones further to the south-east, at Carn Meini (long thought to be a possible source), were probably looking in the wrong place.

route makes much more sense. It is also worth adding that in societies where people move megaliths today, they prefer to avoid risks involving water as far as possible. Megalith-moving is also a thoroughly social activity, rather than just a technical exercise, so going overland would have provided a travelling spectacle to which communities along the route and from beyond would have been drawn. The stones could thus have been relayed from one local group to another through Wales and along the Bristol Avon and River Wylye to Stonehenge.

Stonehenge stage 2 – sarsen trilithons, circle and lintels

The requirements for building stage 2 – the sarsen monument – were very different to those of stage 1. Some 80 very large sarsen stones, weighing between 4 and 40 tons, had to be quarried, roughly shaped and then dragged many miles to Stonehenge. Here, outside its north-east entrance, they were finely dressed with hammerstones, as were some of the bluestones already present within Stonehenge. The sarsen uprights were then raised up in pits dug with antler picks. The stone lintels, weighing 4 tons or more, were raised to the tops of the trilithons and to the top of the outer sarsen circle.

Archaeologists have not yet identified any precise sources for the sarsen stones at Stonehenge. There are fallen standing stones of sarsen in the vicinity of Stonehenge: one of these is the Cuckoo Stone, near Woodhenge, probably erected c 2900 BC. Another is the Bulford Stone, situated east of the River Avon near Durrington Walls. Both of these stones were erected very close to where they had lain naturally, judging by the solution hollows which had formed where they had rested for the previous 55 million years. So could Stonehenge's stones have similarly come from close by on Salisbury Plain? The answer is probably not. The Stonehenge sarsens are mostly very large indeed, much larger than any sarsens that are locally available. Even taking account of the use of sarsen as a building material over many centuries from the Roman period onwards, there is simply not enough broken-up sarsen in the local area. There is no indication from house foundations, walls or field edges on Salisbury Plain that the area ever had copious quantities of sarsen of the right size.

Our best clue about the origins of the Stonehenge sarsens comes from observations made centuries ago by John Aubrey and William Stukeley, long before commercial sarsen-breakers cleared whole landscapes of sarsen boulders. Sarsen stones are found over many parts of southern England, from East Anglia to Dorset and from Kent to Oxfordshire. Yet they are largest and most prolific on the Marlborough Downs, about 20 miles (32km) north of Stonehenge. They were (and still are, in some valleys) so abundant that they resemble grazing flocks of sheep, thereby earning them the name of 'Grey Wethers' [a wether is a castrated ram].

In the mid-17th century John Aubrey reckoned that the Marlborough Downs were where Stonehenge's sarsens came from since they 'are of the very kind of stone with the Grey-weathers about 14 miles off: that tract of ground near Marleborough'. William Stukeley thought similarly:

> In regard to the natural history of these stones, 'tis the same as that of Stonehenge, which is composed of the very same stones, fetched from the same Marlborough downs, where they lie on the surface in great plenty, of all dimensions.

Stukeley had an even more precise idea of where the sarsens came from. Thanks to his careful observations we know that in his day, *c* 1720, the largest sarsen stones could be found not in the valleys (where they survive today) but on top of the downs between the valleys. At Clatford, Stukeley drew and described a group of a dozen sarsen blocks that Aubrey had previously noted were 'rudely hewn'. Stukeley also realised that these were Stonehenge-sized stones:

> Perhaps those were stones going to Stonehenge for they seem to have been brought from the top of the

Figure 4.10
Landscape archaeologists Andrew Fleming and David Field inspecting a sarsen stone on the Marlborough Downs (© Mike Parker Pearson)

hill northward thence where upon a long ridg there are many stones of Vast bulk besides what lye in all the valleys round in great quantity.

More than this, Stukeley reckoned that, on top of the Marlborough Downs, he could still see the pits from which Neolithic quarry workers had extracted the Stonehenge sarsens: 'from the Grey Wethers all [Stonehenge's stones] seem to be fetcht for the holes yet appear whence such were drawn.' One such possible stone-extraction pit, over 100m long, lies on Clatford Down, 2 miles (3.2km) north-west of Clatford, within the middle of the Marlborough Downs, but only archaeological excavation will reveal whether it really is a megalith quarry.

The sarsen stones could have been moved in several ways. A popular notion is that they were transported on wooden tree-trunk rollers, either resting directly on the rollers or sitting on a wooden sledge or cradle. Yet this wouldn't have worked: many of the stones are so heavy that the rollers would have simply embedded themselves in the turf and failed to move. Another frequent suggestion from members of the public is that Neolithic engineers waited for the ground to freeze and then created ice-roads to slide the stones. Sadly for this cunning idea, the Neolithic climate was actually warmer than it is today so the ground would never have been frozen for anything like long enough.

So, wooden rollers and ice-roads may be non-starters, but there are plenty more ideas. Many solutions have been proposed by modern-day engineers and builders; perhaps the most ingenious is the idea that the stones could have been 'rowed'. Two rows of people on either long side of the stone can use wooden levers to lift it off the ground, swing the levers in one direction, moving the stone 15cm in the opposite direction, and then lower it. This action is then repeated countless times as the 'stone-rowers' edge the stone along.

Perhaps the last word on moving large megalithic stones should be left to the ancients themselves. Ancient Egyptian and Mesopotamian bas-reliefs and paintings of people moving large monuments show hundreds of men pulling on a series of ropes, just as one can see in Indonesia or Madagascar today, with the statue or obelisk sitting on a sledge or cradle. In one Egyptian picture, logs can be seen placed in front of the sledge, clearly designed to reduce friction, but mysteriously these logs appear to have been placed longitudinally rather than horizontally as rollers. The reason for this may lie in the depiction of men standing on the front of the sledge and pouring liquids from pots onto the logs. They are almost certainly pouring a lubricant – oil or even just water – onto the logs to allow the sledge to slide on top of them.

In 1996 an experiment was conducted not far from Stonehenge to compare rolling with sliding. A concrete replica of one of the great trilithon's uprights was hauled over log rollers and then on lubricated wooden rails. There was no question about the result: the rails were the easier method.

Erecting the sarsens at Stonehenge presented further challenges. Each stone had to be raised to a vertical position without its base skidding over the hole dug for it. Most of the holes for the sarsens were not very deep – little more than a metre – and without any appreciable ramp to guide the stone into the hole. To prevent the stone's base digging into the side of the hole, a line of anti-friction stakes needed to be positioned along one side of the pit. For large sarsens, experiments have shown that the use of an A-frame allows greater leverage for those pulling on the ropes to lift the stone into place. The giant trilithon uprights are 11m long (though one is now broken in half) and experiments in 1996 with the concrete replica showed that a substantial counterweight was needed to get the base of such a long stone to go easily into its hole. The holes for the great trilithon at Stonehenge are 2.4m deep, far more massive than for the other uprights.

One of the surprises about the erected sarsens is that many are not the neat, rectangular, domino-like blocks that they appear to be above ground. Their bases are irregular, asymmetrical and often pointed: the least aesthetically pleasing ends of the sarsen blocks have been hidden by putting those ends in the ground. This must have made erection even more difficult and it certainly has not helped their stability because, over the years, many of the sarsens have fallen down and, in some cases, have been put back up in recent times.

What stirs the public imagination more than any other aspect of building Stonehenge is how the stone lintels were raised. Lifting a 4-ton stone up

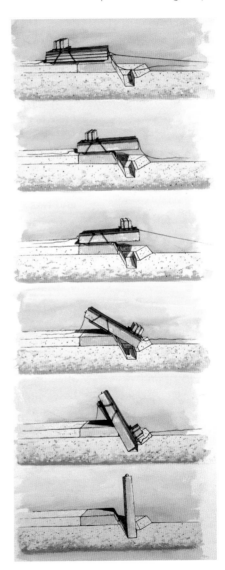

Figure 4.11
Suggested method of erecting a large sarsen stone drawn by Peter Dunn (© Historic England)

to 9m into the air and then aligning its two mortise holes into two projecting tenons on the tops of two adjacent uprights is an extraordinary achievement for a society with simple technology. Just how did they do it?

One possibility is that they used the methods employed by present-day dolmen builders when raising a capstone. The Sumba islanders of Indonesia do this with a ramp of wooden scaffolding and hundreds pulling the stone up the ramp to the right height. A similar approach would be to construct a ramp of earth: it is possible that this was the method used to raise the huge capstones onto Pembrokeshire dolmens such as Garn Turne and Pentre Ifan. Such a method would have enabled the capstone to be pulled into position and, as the soil was carefully removed, so the capstone would gently settle into position. The soil could then be removed from the chamber and from around the dolmen and taken elsewhere to be dumped.

A similar method using an earthen or chalk ramp could well have been used at Stonehenge but there is no indication of the likely source of such a huge mound of chalk and soil, or its eventual place of disposal. The 1996 experiments included raising the lintel of a concrete great trilithon by rocking it on a cradle of wooden sleepers; one end was raised and a beam was placed under it, then the other end was raised and another beam placed under that end, and so on – a technique known as 'jack and pack'. The trickiest part was at the end, when the lintel had to be tilted and slid into position above the tenons before being lowered so that the tenons fitted snugly into the mortise holes.

Figure 4.12
Suggested method of raising a lintel stone into position drawn by Peter Dunn (© Historic England)

Precision was extremely important because the lintels had to fit perfectly. The now-fallen lintel of the great trilithon reveals that these Neolithic engineers did not always get it right. Two sets of mortise holes have been carved, one on the top side and one on the bottom. It is clear that a mistake was made in the size and spacing of one pair, so the stone had to be flipped over and its holes carved out again on the other side.

Building Stonehenge

Figure 4.13 *Cleaning a bluestone lintel stone in 1954. Note the well-made mortise holes for the tenons on the uprights. This lintel today remains buried at Stonehenge (Reproduced by permission of Historic England)*

Figure 4.14 *The tenons on a sarsen upright (Stone 10)*

Measuring out the monument

Archaeologists and scientists have wondered for years how the monument was laid out and to what degree of accuracy. William Stukeley reckoned that the unit of measurement used by prehistoric engineers at Stonehenge was not the Roman foot (which we know measured *c* 0.96 statute feet or 0.293m) and that therefore the monument dated to before the Romans came to Britain. In contrast, Flinders Petrie measured the internal diameter of the sarsen circle as being exactly 100 Roman feet, although his version of the Roman foot was 0.973 statute feet. During the 1960s, Alexander Thom, a retired professor of engineering, formulated a unit of measurement (2.72 statute feet or 0.83m) that he called the 'Megalithic Yard', which he deduced was in widespread use for constructing stone monuments from northern Scotland to southern England.

Thom's scheme worked well for numerous Scottish stone circles but did not fit Stonehenge particularly closely. Most dimensions came out as uneven numbers or fractions of his 'megalithic yard' and his 'megalithic rod' (2½ megalithic yards), not regularities and multiples of round numbers. For example, the Aubrey Hole circle has a circumference of 131 megalithic rods and a radius of 52 megalithic yards, while the sarsen circle had an outer and inner diameter of 48 and 45 megalithic rods respectively. Most archaeologists now reckon that Thom's megalithic yard is an over-precise version of a common way of laying-out – the approximate length of a human pace – and they suspect that systems of measurement probably varied from one region of Britain to another, just as was the case until the medieval period.

More recently, archaeologists have shown that the plan of Stonehenge can be laid out without any unit of measurement, simply using ropes to make a series of intersecting circles, or by using the sun's shadow and basic counting. Both methods have the beauty of not requiring a system of measurement but they are geometrically complex: the job could have been done much more simply if a standard unit of measurement had been used.

An important breakthrough may have been achieved by Andrew Chamberlain, professor of bioarchaeology at the University of Manchester, who realised that any unit of measurement used by Stonehenge's builders should also have been applied to other contemporary monuments in the locality (such as the timber circles at Durrington Walls) and that the lengths used should not just be in whole numbers of the unit but in multiples of smaller numbers. He also realised that calculations should be made from the centres of postholes or stoneholes, not from the edge of a post or stone, since people laying out a plan on the ground would have indicated where the centre-point of each post or stone should go and thus where its hole should be dug.

Chamberlain discovered that the outer four rings of wooden posts of the Durrington Walls' Southern Circle had diameters of approximately 70, 90, 110 and 120 'long feet' (1.056 statute feet or 0.32187m). The 'long foot' is an ancient English unit of measurement, just slightly longer than the modern 'statute foot'. Turning to Stonehenge, he found that the diameters of the stage 1 Aubrey Hole ring, bank, ditch and outer bank were 270, 300, 330 and 360 long feet. The diameters were computed in multiples of 30; on the ground, working from the length of a rope to give the radius, the rope could have been knotted at intervals of 15 long feet. At the Southern Circle, the builders were working in multiples of 5 and 10 along the length of their rope.

The diameter of the mid-line of the sarsen circle at Stonehenge – 95.34 long feet – is not a convincing number, because it is a fraction rather than a whole number. At first glance it would seem that the case for the long foot falls down here, but when we examine the length of the circle's circumference rather than its diameter, it turns out to be almost exactly 300 long feet. With 30 uprights and 30 lintels, each lintel length was approximately 10 long feet, thereby giving the Neolithic stone-masons a clear round number to work to.

It might sound strange that Neolithic builders were working to base 5 and base 10 since these seem such modern concepts, embodied in the decimal system that was only introduced comparatively recently to replace a British system of using base 12 in measuring distance (inches in a foot), money (pence in a shilling) and time (hours in a day). Yet 5 and 10 are very obvious choices in a pre-modern society – we are all able to count on our fingers.

Given that simple mathematics was all that was needed for laying-out Stonehenge in its two main stages, what could possibly go wrong? The lintels of the sarsen circle were the problem. As well as having mortise holes, these lintels have dove-tailed ends so that each lintel should have a concave-shaped end and a convex-shaped end to slot into its neighbours. Only five lintels are still in place on the sarsen circle so there isn't a full set to examine, but one of these five was dressed with two convex ends. Nor are all the lintels the precise 10 long feet that they should have been, so there must have been a certain amount of bodging and fudging to get the sarsen circle up. Some of these potential problems could have been addressed when the sarsen stones were being shaped, lying on the ground outside the north of Stonehenge's enclosure. This area would have provided sufficient space to lay out the various uprights and lintels to make sure that they would all ultimately fit together.

Some time may have been required to lay out the monument on its various orientations towards midwinter solstice sunset, midsummer sunrise and, in the case of the Station Stones, southerly major moonrise and northerly major moonset. The solar orientations could be observed in the course of a single year and were, in any case, observable in the direction of the periglacial stripes and ridges that were later incorporated into the Avenue. Recording the moon's full cycle was a much longer process since it takes 18.6 years. There may have been long periods of preparation, over 20 years or so, not just to lay out these orientations but also

Figure 4.15 *The ends of the lintel stones are carefully shaped to fit together*

Building Stonehenge

to arrange the entire project at each stage, co-opting groups from many different regions of Britain and organising the provision of materials, food and labour.

Stonehenge complete?

Whether Stonehenge was ever finished is a vexed question. Today many of the uprights and even more of the lintels are missing from the sarsen circle, especially around the west and south-west sides. In 2013 the dry summer resulted in parch-marks being visible in the grass which indicated the presence of stone-holes in the area where sarsen uprights were previously thought to be missing (see Fig 1.23). The existence of these previously unknown stone-holes, which complete the circle, suggests Stonehenge was indeed finished.

However, there is a 'problem' stone on the south side of the sarsen circle that challenges the idea of the circle's full completion. This is Stone 11 and it is nowhere near tall enough to have supported lintels. It is also scarcely wide enough to have had two tenon knobs on its top, even if it was once taller than it is now. This is curious because the sarsen uprights on each side of it have tenons, in the expectation of holding up lintels shared with Stone 11. Without archaeological excavation at the base of Stone 11, we can only guess at the possibilities. It could have been put up as a deliberately short upright in order to form a southern entrance into the circle, congruent with the south entrance into the larger enclosure. Alternatively, the stone may have been erected at a much later date to replace a fallen or damaged upright.

Stone 11 was dressed no differently from the other uprights of the sarsen circle, except that there was extensive hammering damage to its top. This could have been done most easily when it was lying down at some point after it was initially dressed and erected, but we can't rule out the possibility that someone climbed up there to bash away at it.

A recent study of the surfaces of each and every stone with laser-scanning technology has contributed many insights into how these stones were dressed. The basic tool was the hammerstone, some very large and boulder-sized but most of them fist-sized. Excavation of the sarsen-dressing area north of Stonehenge's enclosure produced 50 hammerstones from an area of just 25 square metres. This means the whole dressing area is likely to contain another 10,000 fist-sized hammerstones. Some hammerstones were used as packing to hold the sarsen uprights in place, while others were simply strewn on the ground, like debris on an unfinished building site.

One of the most interesting deductions from the laser-scanning is that different methods of dressing were used on different sets of standing stones. The trilithon uprights and the inner horseshoe of bluestones were dressed in the same way, with tooling from hammerstones running vertically as well as horizontally on each stone. In contrast, there are no horizontal panels of tooling on the uprights of the sarsen circle. This raises the likelihood that the trilithons and certain of the bluestones were put up first during stage 2 (*c* 2500 BC) and that the sarsen circle was erected in a different operation a few years later (but still in stage 2).

Of course, the bluestones had most probably already been at Stonehenge for 400 years when the sarsens were erected, but the

Figure 4.16 *The odd-size Stone 11*

     Building Stonehenge

Figure 4.17 *Part of the dressing floor excavated in the area to the north of Stonehenge. Inset: some of the many hammerstones recovered*

nineteen bluestones that are shaped may well only have been dressed at this point. It is not surprising that the trilithons and bluestone Q and R Hole setting were put up before the sarsen circle because, logistically, it would have been almost impossible to erect them the other way round. The sarsen circle simply cannot have gone up first as there would have been no room to erect the trilithons inside an already constructed sarsen circle. Thus the trilithons and bluestone Q and R Hole setting could have been put up as much as a century or so before the sarsen circle. Unfortunately the wide range on the radiocarbon date from the one antler pick from a trilithon stone-hole does not allow a closer dating of this event.

Figure 5.1
Stonehenge memorabilia: an early guidebook from 1877 and items from the Wiltshire Museum's collection (© Mike Pitts; Wiltshire Museum, Devizes)

Stonehenge as an antiquity

5

The people who built Stonehenge must have imagined that its message of shared ancestry and eternal unity of people and cosmos would, like its stones, last forever, for future generations to appreciate and understand. Unfortunately for them, the world was changing. Megalith-building was already a thing of the past on the Continent and, excepting a few brief regional revivals, was on its way out in Britain and Ireland too. New people from abroad with new ways of doing things meant that the old ideas of centralised power, large-scale projects, and the collective authority of the ancestors were things of the past.

One area where megalithic traditions continued was in Aberdeenshire: here during the period of Stonehenge's stages 3 and 4, people were building 'recumbent stone circles'. These are

Figure 5.2 The well-preserved recumbent stone circle at Easter Aquorthies, near Inverurie, Aberdeenshire. Several different stone types were used in the circle, including red jasper, pinkish porphyry and red and grey granite, suggesting the stones were carefully selected (© RCAHMS)

circles of standing stones but with one of them lying on its side like an altar. There was a similar fashion for stone circles and chambered cairns in the Clava region of north-east Scotland, and local communities across many parts of Britain, from south-west England and Wales to the Peak District, northern England and Scotland, built small versions of stone circles and put up standing stones during the Early Bronze Age. But all of these ventures were small-scale, each involving little more effort than building a round barrow.

Stonehenge stage 5, 1600 BC

Stonehenge's final episode of construction was what appears to be an unfinished attempt at re-siting the bluestones in two concentric rings outside the sarsen circle. Someone got as far as digging two circles of pits, known as the Y and Z Holes, and then left them open to be filled with windblown soil (see Fig 1.32). Antlers have been recovered from the Y and Z Holes but most of them have not been used as antler picks, and they may have been heirlooms before their ultimate deposition in these pits. Perhaps they were parts of headgear worn by people in religious ceremonies. While some date to *c* 1900 BC and others to *c* 1800 BC, they may not have been put into the ground until 1600 BC.

Each of these circles has an outer bank of soil around it, but so slight that the earthen rings were only noticed a few years ago. One suggestion is that these banks formed beneath hedges, leading to the rather corny name 'Stonehedge' to describe them. Another possibility is that these banks were formed from the soil dug out of each circle of pits. There is no trace of any other below-ground features in association with these banks, so they are something of a mystery.

Both the Y and Z Holes have a gap or interruption in the circuit at the south-east. This could have been a planned entrance-way into the monument and, if so, it might have had astronomical symbolism. It broadly looks out towards the midwinter solstice sunrise and, slightly south of this, towards the moon's southernmost point for rising (southern major moonrise). It is just possible that this new and final stage of building involved a shift in the monument's more significant alignments.

Stonehenge graffiti

At a similar time to the construction of the Y and Z Holes
(*c* 1750–1500 BC), some of the stones at Stonehenge were carved
with graffiti. Laser-scanning has identified 115 carvings of bronze
axe-heads and three of bronze daggers on five of the sarsen
uprights. We can date these little carvings to this period because
Bronze Age axe-heads and daggers had very distinctive shapes
which changed over time. Apart from the results of pecking with
hammerstones 800 years earlier, when the stones were dressed
before they were erected, these are the *only* carved images at

Figure 5.3 *An example of the Bronze Age graffiti found on several of the stones. On the left is a dagger and on the right is an axe-head*

Figure 5.4 *Many of the stones have visitors' graffiti on them; it is only in recent times that the Bronze Age graffiti has been recognised*

Stonehenge. Over the years there have been all sorts of claims that one can see carvings of goddesses, phalluses, human faces and so on, but the laser-scanning analysis has shown all of these to be in the minds of the observer and not on the rock after all.

There are some interesting patterns in terms of where the axe-head and dagger carvings are located. Two of the daggers are carved on Stone 53, one of the trilithon uprights, and another is carved on the south side of Stone 23. A line traced from this side of Stone 23 to the north side of Stone 53 gives an astronomical orientation towards southern major moonrise. Conversely, the other direction is oriented on northern major moonset. Apart from trilithon Stone 53, all the axe-heads are carved on the outsides of Stones 3, 4 and 5 on the east side of the sarsen circle, broadly towards the direction of the rising sun around the equinoxes.

One place to see carved Bronze Age axe-heads and daggers close-up is in the British Museum, on a large block of stone found in a round barrow at Badbury in Dorset. The discovery was made long ago so little is known of its context, but there are further examples in western Scotland, among the round cairns at Kilmartin where these carvings adorned the slabs and capstones of burial chambers. It thus seems likely that these carvings were linked to the dead. Perhaps the carvings are the result of a brief fashion during the 900-year long period of burying the dead in round barrows near Stonehenge for commemorating or tallying a death with a carving.

Figure 5.5 Another example of Bronze Age graffiti, here at the Ri Cruin cairn in the Kilmartin valley, Argyllshire. The slab, decorated with seven pecked axe-heads, formed part of a cist (© RCAHMS)

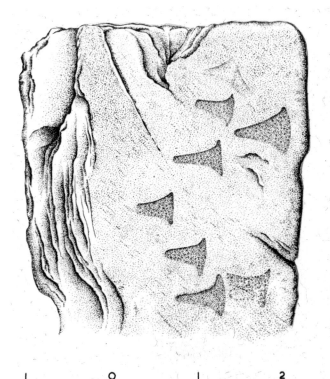

Stonehenge as an antiquity

Stonehenge as an ancient monument

By 1500 BC the landscape around Stonehenge was being divided up by the ditches of land boundaries. After millennia of this landscape being a place for the dead, it was now a farmed landscape of the living. Stonehenge was left alone in its own parcel of land but it was now an ancient monument, out of pace with the times.

People did still visit Stonehenge sporadically: broken pieces of Bronze and Iron Age pots have been found, and in the late Roman period it may even have become a shrine, as numerous pits were dug throughout its interior and coins were scattered about. After the Romans left Britain in AD 410, the monument may have had a rather darker use in the Saxon period – the so-called Dark Ages. Around AD 650 the corpse and head of a decapitated man were buried at Stonehenge, while further fragments of human bone from *c* AD 400 and AD 800 could derive from other executions. It is not impossible that Stonehenge's name derives from 'stone hangings' in Old English, a ready-made gallows for the condemned. However, it is more likely that the name describes stones 'hanging' in the air.

The first written reference to Stonehenge occurs *c* AD 1130, during the reign of Henry I, when there is a brief mention in Henry of Huntingdon's *History of the English*. Henry, archdeacon of Lincoln, says (in Latin) of *Stanenges*: 'No one can work out how the stones were so skilfully lifted up to such a height or why they were erected'. It has been claimed recently that Stonehenge was first mentioned in a land charter dating to AD 937 but this reference to 'Stanheyeg' is a mistake, caused by someone misreading the words *stan hrycg* ('stone ridge'), a feature in the parish of Burcombe many miles to the south of Stonehenge.

Soon after Henry of Huntingdon, *c* 1136, Geoffrey of Monmouth had much to say in his *History of the Kings of Britain* about Stonehenge's building by Merlin, including his unverified assertion that King Aurelius and Uther Pendragon, uncle and father of King Arthur, Britain's favourite mythical king, were buried here.

The first known drawing of Stonehenge is a small illustration from the *Scala Mundi*, a manuscript written *c* 1441 which is kept at Douai in France. This crude sketch shows just four trilithons in a circle, and it is not until 1574 that the first accurate drawing of Stonehenge – a watercolour by Lucas de Heere – was produced.

At the beginning of what we call the modern age, Stonehenge emerged from oblivion and obscurity to become something of

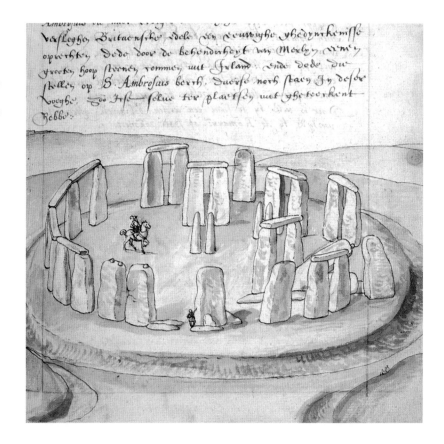

a wonder for a nation beginning to search for its distant past.
Stonehenge featured in William Camden's *Britannia*, a historical
and topographical survey first published in 1586, and in the 1600
edition he described it as 'a huge and monstrous piece of worke',
noting also that 'men's bones have many times been digged up
here ... Ashes and pieces of burnt bone here frequently found'.
Camden was probably talking about bones found in the Bronze
Age burial mounds that surround the stone circle. Not long after,
in 1620, the first excavation was carried out within Stonehenge
itself. The excavation team was led by King James I, who was
accompanied by the Earl of Pembroke, the Duke of Buckingham,
William Harvey (later famous for his study of the circulation
of the blood) and the architect Inigo Jones. They found skulls
of cattle 'or other beasts' and 'great quantities of burnt Coals or
Charcoals' but little else.

These early diggings into buried layers must have caused
unrecorded damage that modern archaeologists can only
guess at. Fortunately, later investigators were more interested

Prospect of STONEHENGE *from the Southwest.*

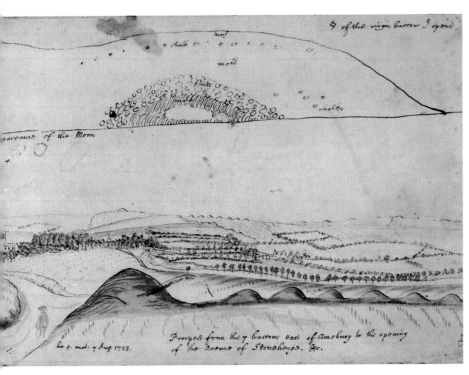

Figure 5.7 *An illustration from William Stukeley's book of 1740 entitled* Stonehenge: a temple restor'd to the British druids *(© Harvard University Library)*

Figure 5.8 *An extract from Stukeley's field notes, dated 7 August 1723, recording his excavation of a round barrow near Stonehenge. This is the first known example of an archaeological section drawing (© Bodleian Library; MS Gough maps 229 f45r)*

Stonehenge as an antiquity

in surveying Stonehenge than digging holes in it. The king's antiquary, John Aubrey, drew a plan of it in the 1660s and, later on, William Stukeley spent many years studying Stonehenge and its surrounding monuments, eventually publishing a book called *Stonehenge: a temple restor'd to the British druids* in 1740.

King James' delving, John Aubrey's drawings, and plans drawn by the 17th-century architect Inigo Jones all reveal the awakening of an analytical interest in Stonehenge and its place in Britain's lengthening ancient past. Stonehenge became a subject for artists and painters from David Loggan to J M W Turner, and people also carved their names and initials into the stones – one of these (who made the mark '+ WREN') may actually have been local lad Christopher Wren, later to design St Paul's Cathedral in London. By the early 19th century visitors had started to arrive in large numbers, with local shops in Amesbury selling hammers for those wanting to take away a souvenir of Stonehenge. Many of these rock-hunting visitors were apparently convinced – perhaps from reading Geoffrey of Monmouth's ancient text – that pieces of stone from the monument had special healing powers.

During the 19th century antiquarianism developed into the science of archaeology and there were further investigations of Stonehenge, beginning with Sir Richard Colt Hoare and William Cunnington who excavated a few small trenches there at the beginning of the century. Between 1874 and 1880 William Flinders Petrie, then a young man who would go on to become the so-called 'Father of Egyptology', accurately mapped the stones and gave them the numbering system still used today. Even the naturalist Charles Darwin dug at Stonehenge, using the opportunity of a family picnic in 1877 to dig holes against two of the stones. This was not, however, out of any archaeological interest but to demonstrate the remarkable power of earthworms for working and developing soil.

Stonehenge in the 20th century

Stonehenge remained in private hands until 1918, owned by the Antrobus family. Sir Edmund Antrobus (the 3rd baronet) was opposed to excavation at Stonehenge and turned down requests from archaeologists such as Petrie to work there. But in 1899 an upright stone and lintel fell down, and another stone – the surviving upright of the great trilithon – was leaning perilously. In 1901, the 4th baronet (also named Sir Edmund) agreed to this stone being lifted and reset. This work required archaeological excavation, which was carried out by William Gowland, an elderly professor of geology with considerable experience of archaeology in Japan and Korea.

Gowland was a good excavator and he published his results promptly in 1902. Sad to say, his exact and innovative method of three-dimensional recording of artefacts was not employed by the next archaeologists who dug within Stonehenge in the 20th century. The first of these was William Hawley, a retired lieutenant-colonel, who dug almost the entire eastern half of Stonehenge between 1919 and 1926 with his assistant Robert Newall, publishing a series of interim reports as he went. Professor Richard Atkinson, accompanied by Professor Stuart Piggott and local archaeologist J F S Stone, carried out major works at various times between 1950 and 1978, and while Atkinson

Figure 5.9 *William Hawley and his excavation team in the 1920s. Hawley is the gentleman seated on the right, with the moustache and flat cap (Reproduced by permission of Historic England)*

wrote an excellent popular book on Stonehenge, published in 1956 and updated in 1979, he never managed to publish his full results in any detail. Only in 1995 were the results of these 20th-century excavations finally brought together and published by Rosamund Cleal and her colleagues at the Trust for Wessex Archaeology. Critically, this work was accompanied by a new programme of radiocarbon dating which provided definitive evidence of the Late Neolithic date of the main stone settings.

Like the antiquarians of previous centuries, Hawley and Atkinson focused on the monument itself, but by the later 20th century archaeologists had begun to think about the landscape around it. In 1979 the Royal Commission on Historical Monuments published the results of their survey of the area around Stonehenge, recording hundreds of prehistoric monuments in its vicinity. Eleven years later, Julian Richards, archaeologist and broadcaster, published the full results of his *Stonehenge Environs Project*, revealing that the land around Stonehenge had been densely occupied during prehistory. Archaeologists were now re-directing their investigations to the Neolithic landscape and the people who lived and died there.

Repairs and restoration

William Gowland's excavation in 1901, a small trench dug around the leaning upright (Stone 56) of the great trilithon, was the first concerted piece of research to accompany restoration of the monument. In 1797 another of the trilithons (Stones 57 and 58) had fallen down and, a hundred years later, other stones were being propped up with wooden poles. In 1900 Stone 22 in the sarsen circle fell down. After the monument passed into public ownership in 1918, Hawley's excavations between 1919 and 1926 accompanied a major programme of repair, re-erecting fallen stones and consolidating those most likely to topple. In 1958 Atkinson's excavations accompanied the Ministry of Works' re-erection of Stone 22, and Stones 57 and 58 of the fallen trilithon. Stone 23 fell in 1963 and was put back up in 1964, at the same time as Stones 27 and 28 were straightened and the re-erected trilithon of Stones 57 and 58 was also re-set.

Not everyone has shared this appreciation of Stonehenge: a military airfield was built during the First World War in the field immediately west of Stonehenge and rumours circulated that staff of the Royal Flying Corps wanted it torn down so as not to impede low-flying planes. In more recent times, the amount of remedial work has worried some people, since Stonehenge has been substantially reconstructed. One April Fool's Day-style press spoof claimed that Stonehenge is not prehistoric at all but is a modern fake!

Figure 5.10 *Professor Richard Atkinson excavating at Stonehenge on behalf of the Ministry of Works in 1958. Behind him is Professor Stuart Piggott. Note the wooden scaffolding around the adjacent sarsen (Reproduced by permission of Historic England)*

Peopling the landscape – past and present

The astronomical significance of Stonehenge has been recognised since the 19th century but it was only in the 1960s that the wider public became aware of such matters. In 1965 the astronomer Gerald Hawkins published his 'decoding' of Stonehenge, interpreting it as a prehistoric computer for calculating lunar and solar eclipses as well as the midsummer and midwinter solstices and other astronomical phenomena. Astronomer Fred Hoyle produced a similar interpretation, and retired engineer Alexander Thom applied his concept of the 'megalithic yard', a unit of measurement that he thought was used by Britain's megalith builders, to Stonehenge's dimensions.

Figure 5.11 *Druids celebrating at Stonehenge in 1982 (© Mike Pitts)*

Stukeley's idea that Stonehenge was a temple for Iron Age druids was now replaced by notions of Neolithic astronomer-priests using the monument as an astronomical observatory to calculate festival calendars. In 1977, archaeologist Euan MacKie suggested that these priests had lived nearby, within the great henge of Durrington Walls. Such interpretations chimed with growing popular interest in Stonehenge as it became a site for free festivals each midsummer, when thousands gathered to await the sunrise. The great stone circle was an icon of the growing counter-culture within 1970s' Britain, the focus of a multitude of enthusiasts' theories about UFOs, ley lines, hidden energy forces and lost mysticism.

Figure 5.12
Thousands gather to celebrate the midsummer sunrise in the late 1990s, when Stonehenge was once again open to the public at the solstice (© Mike Pitts)

In 1985 the Stonehenge free festival was cancelled by the police, who asked festival-goers not to gather there at midsummer. Among those who tried to reach the stones in spite of a police blockade were the 'peace convoy' of New-Age travellers who were brutally attacked in a heavy-handed police operation subsequently known as the 'Battle of the Beanfield'. For the next ten years Stonehenge was off limits to midsummer revellers.

Since those dark days, the different parties have come to some degree of reconciliation but Stonehenge remains a contested place. Archaeologists have also returned to Stonehenge and its landscape, bringing old records up to date, developing research frameworks for the future, and embarking on new and ground-breaking research that has transformed our understanding of who built Stonehenge, how, when and why.

Working in the Stonehenge landscape

The last of Richard Atkinson's excavations at Stonehenge was in 1978, and except for a few small development-related projects, such as Mike Pitts' excavation in advance of a cable trench beside the Heel Stone in 1980, the only large-scale investigation during the 1980s was Julian Richards' *Stonehenge Environs Project*. The last 40 years have seen major changes in the management of the Stonehenge landscape, not least its inscription in 1986, along with Avebury, on the list of World Heritage Sites, such that it is now

Figure 5.13 *For many years there were calls for the A344 road alongside Stonehenge to be closed, and these intensified after it became a World Heritage Site in 1986. The passing traffic, including military vehicles, seriously detracted from the experience of visiting the site, but it was not until 2013 that the road was finally closed*

one of the most heavily protected areas in England; this makes carrying out any form of archaeological investigation quite a challenge.

Nearly twenty years passed after the completion of the *Stonehenge Environs Project* before another major research project on Stonehenge was launched in 2003. This was the *Stonehenge Riverside Project* (SRP), led by Mike Parker Pearson and colleagues Josh Pollard, Colin Richards, Julian Thomas, Chris Tilley and Kate Welham from a consortium of British universities' archaeology departments. Excavations carried out by the SRP at a number of locations within the WHS have radically transformed our understanding of the area in the 3rd millennium BC.

The Stonehenge World Heritage Site (WHS) covers an area of 2665ha (26.6km²) and within that area lie more than 350 known burial mounds and other prehistoric sites. The land is owned by several major bodies such as English Heritage, the National Trust and the Ministry of Defence, as well as private individuals, and various parts of the landscape are protected by designations ranging from Scheduled Monument to Special Landscape Area. The WHS is managed by a committee with representatives from numerous national and local bodies, such as Natural England, the Highways Department and local councils.

In 2010, planning permission was finally granted for the closure of the A344 road adjacent to Stonehenge, demolition of the 20th-century car park and buildings, and the construction of a new visitor centre at Airman's Corner, 1½ miles (2.5km) to the

north-west of the monument. The closure of the road in 2013 has reunited the monument with its surrounding landscape and it is now possible to walk from Stonehenge to Durrington Walls, via other monuments such as the Greater Cursus and the Avenue.

Permission to excavate within the WHS area is only granted in exceptional circumstances, when important questions cannot be answered without digging. The recent *Stonehenge Hidden Landscapes* project used a variety of remote-sensing methods to obtain as much information as possible from the landscape without any form of excavation, while the *Stonehenge Riverside Project* (SRP) (see pp 136–9) carried out a number of excavations, small and large, both within the monument and in the surrounding area.

Excavations at Stonehenge itself are today very rare, but in 2008 permission was granted for two trenches. The first of these was dug by Tim Darvill and Geoff Wainwright as part of their *SPACES* project (Strumble-Preseli Ancient Communities and Environment Study) which was investigating possible sources for the bluestones in Pembrokeshire. The purpose was to find out when the bluestones were erected within the Q and R Holes (inside the sarsen circle

Figure 5.14 *Since the closure of the A344 in 2013, the road has been returned to grassland. The new Visitor Centre at Airman's Corner opened in December 2013*

Stonehenge Riverside Project 2003–2009

The SRP set out initially to investigate the river-based relationship between Stonehenge and Durrington Walls, but over seven seasons of work, the team carried out excavations at a number of sites across the Stonehenge landscape. Excavations started at Durrington Walls in 2004 and, within the next three years, revealed the presence of many houses both underneath the banks of the henge as well as in its centre. An entirely unknown ceremonial, solstice-aligned avenue was also found, running from the previously excavated Southern Circle to the River Avon.

The SRP team partially re-excavated Woodhenge, the timber circle next to Durrington Walls first investigated in 1926–27. Discoveries included the remains of a two-phase stone setting that replaced the circles of timber posts, and an Early Neolithic deposit of pottery under the henge bank. Further south, the team excavated the remains of three more timber-post structures of monumental size and a pit circle, suggesting that this zone of high ground along the riverside was an important location for observing activities on the river below Durrington Walls.

Two standing stones survive in the vicinity of Durrington Walls: the Cuckoo Stone to its south-west and the Bulford Stone to its east. The ground around both of these was excavated and found to have a long history of use, including Early Bronze Age cremation burials. At the Cuckoo Stone, three burials were placed in pottery urns of a type called Collared Urns; at the Bulford Stone, two Food Vessels were buried in a multiple cremation grave with flint arrowheads, tusks of wild boar and other artefacts including a small block of crystal. Activity at the Cuckoo Stone had begun c 2900 BC, probably when the stone was erected, and ended in the Late Roman period when two coin hoards were buried beside the stone; by this time, the Cuckoo Stone had become enveloped within the outskirts of an expanding Roman rural settlement centred on Larkhill.

The SRP team set out to date the Greater Cursus and the long barrow (Amesbury 42) positioned at its east end. Broken antler picks from the base of both the cursus and the long barrow ditches provided radiocarbon

Figure 5.15 *Archaeologists may have many scientific techniques at their disposal in the 21st century, but excavation is still a manual operation. Here a Roman burial of a child with a dog skull near the Cuckoo Stone is recovered*

Figure 5.16 *Site recording utilises both traditional and modern methods. Here Josh Pollard is drawing a section of a ditch to record the different layers of soil with which it filled up in prehistory*

dates which demonstrate that the monuments were built around the same time as the Lesser Cursus, *c* 3500 BC. The excavations here showed that an antler pick found in the ditch of the Greater Cursus in 1947, dating to *c* 2500 BC, had actually been used not in the original construction but in a much later re-digging of the in-filled ditch, in an attempt to reinstate its alignment a thousand years after it was first built. This reinstatement may have coincided with the erection of the sarsen trilithons and outer circle and the re-setting of the bluestones at Stonehenge.

The Stonehenge landscape also contained two undated lengths of ditch that run approximately north-east to south-west to the west of Stonehenge, leaving a wide opening to the north-west of the monument. Known as the Palisade Ditch and the Gate Ditch, these were thought to be Neolithic on account of the wooden palisade that once ran along the bottom of the ditch but the SRP excavations showed them to date to the end of the Early Bronze Age, *c* 1600–1500 BC, perhaps just before the landscape was divided up for fields. Late Bronze Age infant burials in the top of the ditch were accompanied by a beautifully carved little chalk pig.

With the discovery of an avenue linking Durrington Walls to the River Avon, the SRP re-examined the Stonehenge Avenue to see if it too led as far as the river. It had only ever been tracked to within 200m of the river at West Amesbury so there was uncertainty about its full length and whether it was built in different stages at different dates. Excavations at the so-called 'elbow' of the Avenue, where it deviates from its solstice-aligned axis and heads towards King Barrow Ridge and the river, demonstrated that there was no break in the Avenue's construction at that point – the 'elbow' and the section beyond to the river are definitely part of the original layout.

Thus the Avenue was shown to extend to the riverside at West Amesbury, with one of its ditches producing a beautifully pressure-flaked Late Neolithic flint arrowhead of 'oblique' type, dating to 2600–2400 BC. The Avenue, however, stopped just short of the river's edge by about 30m. In this gap lay a previously undiscovered henge monument, about 30m wide with an external bank and a probable east entrance. Built *c* 2400 BC, objects found in its ditch included a specially placed deposit of antler picks and flint and bone tools.

More significantly, this henge (now known as Bluestonehenge) was built to enclose an earlier feature which consisted of a circle of inter-cutting pits, each with a ramp for the insertion of a standing stone into the pit. The impressions made on the bottom of the pits and the voids left by pulling out the stones showed that they were thin pillars, almost certainly bluestones. Only part of the site was excavated, to leave something for future researchers, but we estimate that about 25 bluestone pillars once stood here. Antler picks left in the holes date to *c* 2400 BC, indicating when the stones were removed, but unfortunately nothing from the moment of the circle's construction could be dated except for several flint arrowheads of the 'chisel' type, which were in use broadly in the period 3400–2600 BC.

Closer to Stonehenge, the SRP's excavations revealed a dressing-floor 100m north of the monument's enclosure ditch. Geophysical survey showed that this was just a small part of a fan-shaped spread of sarsen debris that can also be tracked by the distribution of small sarsen chippings found in mole-hills across the field north of Stonehenge. Analysis of the debris revealed a dense spread of sarsen chippings and hammerstones, indicative of the large sarsens being dragged to this area before being carefully shaped prior to erection in the Stonehenge enclosure.

Figure 5.17 *Modern technology makes some aspects of site recording, such as surveying, much easier. This is a laser scanner, used here to record house floor surfaces*

Sarsen debris was also found underneath the banks of the Stonehenge Avenue. This debris demonstrates that the sarsens were brought to Stonehenge before the Avenue was constructed. We now know that the sarsens were put up *c* 2500 BC, that the Avenue's ditches were dug *c* 2400 BC, and that the ditches were cleaned out at least once after that. The excavation trench across the Avenue revealed large and deep periglacial fissures running on the solstice axis. The two natural ridges that acted as a funnel for the fissures could be seen to run for about 150m, fizzling out before the 'elbow' where the Avenue's ditches continued beyond the ends of these ridges.

As discussed in Chapter 2, these natural features with a fortuitous solstice alignment may have played a very important role in determining why Stonehenge was built where it was. Excavations in 2013 by Wessex Archaeology after removal of the tarmac of the A344 beside the Heel Stone revealed these large periglacial fissures again, closer to Stonehenge, demonstrating that they are localised to within the Avenue and do not exist beyond it on either side. The Avenue is deliberately placed right on top of these natural features.

Figure 5.18 *Regular visits by a reconstruction artist during the actual excavation process produce more accurate and meaningful images. This is Peter Dunn's watercolour of the Southern Circle at Durrington Walls. Reconstructions always pose a number of questions: here, Peter has suggested lintels on the circle, as at Stonehenge but in timber, and elaborate decoration on the entrance posts (© Peter Dunn)*

and outside the trilithon horseshoe). Many years earlier Richard Atkinson had concluded that the stones in the Q and R Holes were put up before the sarsen circle but the SPACES excavation showed that Atkinson was wrong about this. He thought that part of a stone-hole for a sarsen cut into a bluestone hole but it was shown that this part of the sarsen hole was probably filled with much later material. Thus the Q and R Holes could be considered contemporary with the sarsen circle and trilithons, dating to c 2500 BC, several centuries earlier than Atkinson thought.

Later in 2008 the SRP carried out a very small excavation within Stonehenge to recover the remains of around 60 cremation burials excavated in 1919–26 by William Hawley. In 1935 Hawley's assistant, Robert Newall, placed all the cremated remains found by Hawley in Aubrey Hole 7. Newall put the bones here because he was worried that no museum would take them; at that time in Britain, cremated human remains were not thought to be of any scientific or educational value. Scientific advances since then have been phenomenal, and these cremated remains are a unique source of information about the people of Stonehenge, so they were retrieved from 'storage' in 2008. Although Newall's colleague, William Young, recorded in his diary that they deposited the cremated bones in four separate sandbags, the archaeologists found the bones to be thoroughly mixed up in a single heap on the bottom of the pit. Painstaking analysis has identified fragments of different bones belonging to at least 26 of the individuals buried at Stonehenge, whose remains can now tell us much about their lives.

Careful excavation of Aubrey Hole 7 also revealed that Hawley and Newall had not done a thorough job. They had missed a cremation burial in a small pit on the west side of this Aubrey Hole and they had also failed to excavate completely all of the chalk filling in its base. This filling was a rock-hard matrix of chalk that had once been packed around an upright pillar standing in the hole. A small spread of crushed chalk indicated that this pillar was heavier than wood, and therefore a standing stone. The size of the Aubrey Hole means that it was a bluestone, not a sarsen. This was further evidence to add to that provided by the dimensions of all the Aubrey Holes that they had once contained bluestones c 2900 BC.

In 2012 the results of a laser-scan survey of all the stones at Stonehenge were interpreted with computerised imaging techniques by ArcHeritage, an archaeological consultancy in Sheffield. Developing new methods of recognising carvings on

the sarsens, they were able to more than double the number of previously known axe-head carvings (see Fig 5.3). They also discovered much about the methods of stone-dressing used by Stonehenge's builders.

Meanwhile English Heritage's own experts have recently completed a study of the earthworks of Stonehenge and its surrounding monuments, including a geophysical survey within Stonehenge. Without having to dig any holes, they have produced results which raise new questions about whether there was an earlier monument under the 'north barrow' on the site of Stonehenge before 2900 BC. They also point to the possibility that several of the round barrows immediately to the south-west of Stonehenge may have started out as earlier monuments such as small long barrows or cremation enclosures.

Figure 5.19 *The array of geophysical equipment used by the* Stonehenge Hidden Landscapes *team (© LBI ArchPro, Geert Verhoeven)*

Geophysical surveys have been carried out in the wider landscape by two more teams. The *Stonehenge Hidden Landscapes* project (2010–14), a collaboration between a team from Birmingham University led by Vince Gaffney and the Ludwig Boltzmann Institute for Archaeological Prospection in Vienna, has surveyed most of the Stonehenge World Heritage Site, discovering many new sites of unknown date or purpose in the vicinity of Stonehenge. Fritz Lüth's German team from the Deutsches Archäologisches Institut in Berlin has worked with Tim Darvill of Bournemouth University to cover much of the same ground.

Since 2009 most of the research on Stonehenge has been taking place in laboratories or as non-intrusive survey. Following on from the SRP, Parker Pearson's team have carried out a laboratory-based project, *Feeding Stonehenge*, to investigate where its resources were obtained and in what seasons. Whilst many resources were sourced locally (such as the flint tools and most of the pottery), the cattle and pigs eaten at the Durrington Walls settlement were brought on the hoof from far and wide to be feasted on, in the case of the pigs during the winter months. The *Feeding Stonehenge* project follows on from the *Beaker People Project*, a study of mobility and diet in Britain in the period 2500–1500 BC, starting when the Bell Beaker culture arrived from Europe.

The most recent research excavations in the Stonehenge area have been those by David Jacques of the University of Buckingham at Blick Mead, close to the River Avon near Amesbury. At the foot of an Iron Age hillfort called Vespasian's Camp, Jacques has discovered a dense deposit of Mesolithic flints and associated animal bones, demonstrating the existence of a long-lived and possibly large Mesolithic occupation site.

One of the big questions about Stonehenge – where the stones came from, when and why – can only really be answered by investigations not at Stonehenge itself but at the rock sources. Most of this work has concentrated on the bluestones, a variety of igneous and sedimentary rocks that appear to have been put up as two stone circles at Stonehenge and West Amesbury as early as 2900 BC. Geologists Rob Ixer and Peter Turner have dismissed the suggested Milford Haven origin for the sandstone Altar Stone and shown it to be of Devonian sandstone, possibly from the Brecon Beacons. Ixer has also worked closely with Richard Bevins on the bluestones, which are of volcanic origin, matching chippings and pillars at Stonehenge with specific outcrops in Pembrokeshire, south Wales. Their results, described in Chapters 3 and 4, have led to the discovery of a megalith quarry at Craig Rhos-y-felin as well as the locations of other quarries at Carn Goedog and Cerrigmarchogion on the north flank of the Preseli mountains.

The early 21st century has seen renewed research interest in Stonehenge from teams across Europe. Using techniques previously unknown, they have ushered in a new era of ground-breaking scientific results that have allowed us to understand Stonehenge and its builders as never before. With the increasing pace of scientific innovations and growing sophistication of archaeological method and theory, it is clear that Stonehenge will continue to reveal its secrets for years to come.

Figure 5.20
Stonehenge, probably the most photographed monument in Britain, will continue to fascinate generations to come

Glossary

6

Barrow A burial mound of soil, turf and subsoil, heaped over a grave. *Long* barrows were built in the Early and Middle Neolithic while *round* barrows were built in the Middle Neolithic and Early Bronze Age.

Bluestone A type of stone found at Stonehenge that has its sources in west Wales. It is a general term for a variety of different rocks, including spotted dolerite, rhyolite, argillaceous tuff and sandstone. The bluestone pillars brought to Stonehenge were mostly about 4m long and 2 tons in weight.

Boreal The vegetational epoch, 8500–7000 BC, when birch forests gave way to hazel and pine in a warming climate, prior to the spread of mixed-oak forest across Britain.

Bronze Age The period, 2200–750 BC, during which bronze was the principal metal in use for tools. Metalworkers learnt to alloy tin and copper to make bronze in the Early Bronze Age (2200–1500 BC).

Causewayed enclosures Earthen enclosures, mostly dating to 3800–3600 BC in the Early Neolithic (4000–3500 BC). They were created by digging ditches with gaps or causeways being left in place between each section of ditch.

Cist A small box-like chamber, normally below ground and formed from stone slabs, constructed to contain a corpse or other human remains.

Copper Age The period, 2500–2200 BC, when the first metals were introduced to Britain.

Cursus monuments Long, narrow rectangular enclosures, dating to 3600–3200 BC, surrounded by a ditch and a bank, sometimes miles long. They were built at the end of the Early Neolithic and in the Middle Neolithic (3500–3000 BC).

Disarticulated human bones When a corpse has fully decayed, the bones of the skeleton can separate from each other. Neolithic burial practices included the deliberate disarticulation of skeletons, sometimes involving defleshing.

Dolmen A type of megalith, called a cromlech in Wales, formed from three or more uprights covered by a capstone. These are common in western Britain and Ireland. Portal dolmens have the appearance of an entrance to the dolmen.

Druids Ritual and judicial specialists in Britain at the time of Julius Caesar's invasion in 55 BC. They were first connected to Stonehenge in the 17th and 18th centuries by the antiquarians John Aubrey and William Stukeley because they did not realise the true age of Stonehenge.

Equinox Halfway between the solstices, the sun rises precisely in the east and sets precisely in the west twice a year, around 20 March and 22 September. Unlike the solstices, equinox sunrise and sunset do not seem to have been important at Stonehenge or at other Neolithic monuments.

Fieldwalking A form of archaeological survey involving walking across ploughed fields to plot the distribution of finds (worked flints, pottery sherds *etc*) on the ground surface.

Henge A circular earthwork enclosure (with one, two or four entrances) in which the bank has been built outside the ditch. Although it is the origin of this term, Stonehenge is not a henge; this type of circular earthwork enclosure, with the ditch outside the bank, is known as a 'formative' henge, since it dates to before classic henges.

Holocene The current geological epoch, which follows the last Ice Age.

Lintel A stone block set horizontally on two stone uprights, like the top of a doorway. Stonehenge is the only megalithic monument to have had lintels, set on top of the trilithons and sarsen circle.

Megalith A large stone deliberately set up (normally standing but sometimes laid flat or recumbent) or intended to be set up. Megalithic monuments, comprising one or more megaliths, were built 4700–1500 BC in western Europe. They are erected in numerous societies today.

Menhir A large, upright standing stone, often found singly but sometimes with others.

Mesolithic The Middle Stone Age, *c* 10,000–4000 BC, after the last Ice Age. Britain was still joined to the European mainland at this time and people lived by hunting wild animals and gathering plant foods.

Neolithic The New Stone Age, *c* 4000–2500 BC, when farming was introduced to Britain and people began to live in permanent settlements.

Passage graves Also known as passage tombs, these generally circular tombs of the Early and Middle Neolithic have a long passage leading to a central chamber. In the British Isles, they are found only in Ireland and western Britain.

Radiocarbon dating The scientific method of dating carbon by measuring the decay of the carbon-14 isotope.

Sarsen A silcrete formed of sand and cemented silica 55 million years ago on top of the chalk beds of southern England. As a type of sandstone, it is unusually hard. Most of Stonehenge's stones, including all the large ones, are sarsens.

Solstice The sun rises and sets at its extreme positions twice a year around 21 June and 21 December, the longest and shortest days of the year. The midwinter sun rises in the south-east and sets in the south-west, and the midsummer sun rises in the north-east and sets in the north-west.

Trilithon Two standing stones, joined across the top by a stone lintel. These are known only from Stonehenge where five of them form a horseshoe plan at the centre of the monument.

Acknowledgements 7

The Stonehenge Riverside Project was funded by the Arts and Humanities Research Council, the National Geographic Society, the Natural Environment Research Council, the British Academy, the Society of Antiquaries, the Royal Archaeological Institute, the Robert Kiln Trust and Andante Travel.

Over the years, many people have contributed to archaeological knowledge about Stonehenge. As well as all those that helped us on the Stonehenge Riverside Project, many colleagues have made their own contributions in recent years to our knowledge of this remarkable monument. Some of them are: Marcus Abbott, Mike Allen, Hugo Anderson-Whymark, Martyn Barber, Barbara Bender, Richard Bevins, Mark Bowden, Richard Bradley, Aubrey Burl, Ros Cleal, Vicki Cummings, Tim Darvill, David Field, Andrew Fitzpatrick, Charly French, Vince Gaffney, Julie Gardiner, Paul Garwood, Alex Gibson, Catriona Gibson, Mark Gillings, Jan Harding, Phil Harding, Frances Healy, Rob Ixer, David Jacques, Andy Lawson, Jim Leary, Neil Linford, Chris Moore, Stuart Needham, Andy Payne, Nick Pearce, Mike Pitts, Julian Richards, Clive Ruggles, Rob Scaife, Rick Schulting, Christope Snoeck, Geoff Wainwright, Alasdair Whittle and Ann Woodward.

Together with us on the Stonehenge Riverside Project and follow-up investigations (Feeding Stonehenge Project and Stones of Stonehenge Project) we have been fortunate to work with a great team of hundreds of archaeologists, scientists and students. We particularly thank: Umberto Albarella, Louise Austin, Olaf Bayer, Wayne Bennett, Chris Casswell, Andrew Chamberlain, Ben Chan, Lesley Chapman, Ralph Collard, Christie Cox Willis, Oliver Craig, Glyn Davies, Jolene Delbert, Roger Doonan, Mark Dover, Dave Durkin, Fiona Eaglesham, Jane Evans, Jane Ford,

Abby George, Martin Green, Jim Gunter, Derek Hamilton, Barney Harris, Ian Heath, C J Hyde, Mandy Jay, Kate MacDonald, Richard MacPhail, Pete Marshall, Jacqueline McKinley, Claudia Minniti, Neil Morris, Bob Nunn, Eileen Parker, Alistair Pike, Derek Pitman, Megan and David Price, Becca Pullen, Dave Robinson, Jim Rylatt, Duncan Schlee, Jean-Luc Schwenninger, Dave Shaw, Lawrence Shaw, Pat Shelley, Lisa Shillito, Ellen Simmons and Dave Cooper, Dan Stansbie, Charlene Steele, Susan Stratton, Anne Teather, Lizzie and James Thompson, Chris Tilley, Mike Tizzard, Christina Tsoraki, Sarah Viner-Daniels, Helen Wickstead and Elizabeth Wright.

We are very grateful to the many landowners around Stonehenge and in Pembrokeshire who have allowed us to work on their land, notably Andrew and Meryl Ainslie, Sir Edward and Lady Antrobus, Richard Bawden, Stuart Crook, Huw and Dilys Davies, the Davies brothers and family, John Gale, Alexander Hawkesworth, Billy King, Hugh Morrison, Jack and David Oliver, Vivian and Doreen Phillips, Stan and Henry Rawlins, Geraint Rees, Gill Richards, Mike and Charles Rowland, Phil Sawkill, Anthony Thomas, Robert Turner, Mark Upton and Elaine Williams. Local help and support were provided by Paul and Margot Adams, Steve Dodds, Reg Jury, the Massey family and many, many others. Many institutions were also involved in providing permissions and we thank their representatives for their constructive input: Harriet Attwood, Dave Batchelor, Isabelle Bedu, Phil Bennett, Martin Brown, Peter Carson, Amanda Chadburn, Pete Crane, Lucy Evershed, Rachel Foster, Chris Gingell, Kath Graham, Polly Groom, Richard Osborne and Martin Papworth.

We would like to thank the staff of all the local and national archives which have assisted with images for this book, and in particular: Mike Allen, Andy Chapman, Tim Darvill, David Dawson, Ian Dennis, David Jacques, Nicky Milner, Mike Pitts, Francis Pryor, Henry Rothwell, Chris Scarre and Ken Williams.

Finally, special thanks go to the book's editor, Catrina Appleby, for her hard work and dedication in getting this book ready for publication.

The authors and illustrators 8

Mike Parker Pearson

Mike Parker Pearson is Professor of British Later Prehistory at the Institute of Archaeology, University College London (UCL) and a Fellow of the British Academy. After gaining a BA in European Archaeology at Southampton University in 1979, he was awarded a PhD at Cambridge University in 1985. He worked as an Inspector of Ancient Monuments for English Heritage until 1990. From then on, he lectured in the Department of Archaeology & Prehistory at Sheffield University where he was given a professorial chair in 2005, which he held until moving to UCL in 2012.

Mike has been interested in archaeology since he was four years old. He began his career by taking part in archaeological excavations in southern England from 1972 onwards and has worked on archaeological sites around the world in Denmark, Germany, Greece, Syria, the United States, Madagascar, Rapa Nui (Easter Island) and the Outer Hebrides. He has published nineteen books and many scientific papers. In 2010 he was voted the UK's 'Archaeologist of the Year' and in 2011 he was awarded the Samuel H Kress Lectureship in Ancient Art by the American Institute of Archaeology. Mike first visited Stonehenge when he was just a year old, though his earliest memories of it are as a student and free-festival goer in the 1970s.

Joshua Pollard

Josh is a Reader in Archaeology at the University of Southampton. As a small boy, Josh dug exploratory holes in the family garden, later developing this into an interest in archaeology. He studied for a BA in Archaeology and PhD at Cardiff University, before working as a Project Officer for the Cambridge Archaeological Unit, and subsequently holding posts at Queen's University, Belfast; the University of Wales, Newport; Bristol University; and now the University of Southampton.

Josh has worked on numerous archaeological projects in the UK, and assisted on others in Nepal, Hungary, Romania and Rapa Nui (Easter Island). He has published widely on topics mostly relating to British later prehistory. An abiding interest in the monumental, and love of the chalk downlands of Wessex, has led to him spending more research time in the Avebury and Stonehenge landscapes than is healthy.

Colin Richards

Colin is Professor of Archaeology at the University of Manchester. After starting out as a carpet fitter and TV repairman in Salisbury, he discovered archaeology through evening classes and, as a mature student, took a degree in archaeology at Reading University. It was there that his fascination with the British Neolithic fully developed. Colin was awarded a PhD for his research into Neolithic Orkney at Glasgow University where he was appointed lecturer in archaeology. He later took up a post at the University of Manchester.

Colin's initial interest in archaeology developed from his fascination with Durrington Walls and its Grooved Ware pottery. Since then he has worked on archaeological projects in many parts of the UK. He is director of an excavation project on Rapa Nui (Easter Island) and is an expert on the archaeology of Polynesia. Most of his British fieldwork has been in Orkney where he has excavated numerous Neolithic houses and other sites including Maes Howe tomb and the Ring of Brodgar stone circle. His most recent book, detailing his excavation findings at Calanais, Brodgar and other stone circles, is *Building the Great Stone Circles of the North*. He is currently researching dolmens in Wales and Ireland.

The authors and illustrators

Julian Thomas

Julian is Professor of Archaeology at the University of Manchester. He studied archaeology at Bradford University and gained a PhD at Sheffield University in 1986 on the archaeology of Neolithic southern England. Julian taught archaeology at Lampeter University and Southampton University before being appointed to the chair of archaeology at Manchester in 2000. He has been Secretary of the World Archaeological Congress and is Vice-President of the Royal Anthropological Institute.

Julian has been involved with field archaeology throughout his career, and has directed projects investigating Neolithic ceremonial complexes in Scotland and Herefordshire. As a student, Julian dug on the causewayed enclosure at Crickley Hill in Gloucestershire, inspiring a life-long interest in the British Neolithic. He has published eleven books including, most recently, *The Birth of Neolithic Britain: an interpretive account*.

Kate Welham

Kate Welham is Professor of Archaeological Sciences in the Department of Archaeology, Anthropology and Forensic Science at Bournemouth University. Kate started her academic career outside archaeology, completing a BSc (Hons) in Applied Chemistry. Whilst studying for her chemistry degree Kate was given the opportunity to analyse a variety of artefacts from shipwrecks found around the south coast of England, and it was this early work that started her fascination with all aspects of archaeological science. In 1996 Kate joined the University of Sheffield, and was awarded an MSc and PhD for the scientific study of ancient materials including glass, ceramics and metals.

Kate joined Bournemouth University in 2001, with her career diversifying into archaeological prospection. Her primary research focus is now the application of remote sensing techniques in an archaeological context, and she is an experienced archaeological surveyor with expertise in topographical survey, geophysical prospection, GIS, and 3D scanning technology. Kate has been involved with many archaeological projects across the globe, and has directed a number of recent archaeological surveys on both prehistoric and historic landscapes including Stonehenge, Rapa Nui (Easter Island) and Tanzania.

Irene de Luis de la Cruz

Irene de Luis de la Cruz is a freelance archaeological illustrator. She gained a degree in Archaeological Conservation at Madrid's ESCRBC (Escuela Superior de Conservación y Restauración de Bienes Culturales) in 1994 and a BA in Archaeology at the Complutense University of Madrid in 1998.

She has been interested in art and archaeology since an early age. She has worked as an illustrator for many different archaeological projects in Spain, Syria and Madagascar. In 2010 she published *Dibujo de campo y topografía para arqueólogos*, a book about site illustration and surveying for archaeologists in Spain.

Peter Dunn

Peter Dunn is a freelance archaeological reconstruction artist from Stoke-on-Trent, in the Potteries. A descendant of coal-miners, potters and artists, his grandfather and great-grandfather were skilled artists/designers of decorated ceramics. Peter has always been fascinated by ancient history – the Greek Heroes, the Trojan War, battles, dark towers and King Arthur. His favourite film as a child was *Jason and the Argonauts* with Ray Harryhausen's 'stop-motion' animated figures of titans, harpies and skeleton warriors. Watching TV programmes on Stonehenge, Silbury Hill, ancient Egypt and the Maya got him hooked on archaeology. After gaining a degree in illustration in 1977, Peter had hopes of painting science-fiction book covers but it never quite happened; instead, he took jobs as an illustrator and designer in Stoke and the Yorkshire Dales, later becoming a country park warden in Pembrokeshire, west Wales.

Peter worked as an artist and illustrator for English Heritage from 1985 to 2008, and has been involved in artistic and interpretive projects throughout England as well as abroad. Through archaeological illustrations, reconstruction paintings and drawings of the Neolithic – particularly the monuments and landscape of Stonehenge and Durrington Walls – Peter considers that he has become involved in something far more exciting and awesome, probably the most engrossing subject of all.

Adam Stanford

Adam Stanford is an archaeological photographer specialising in aerial photography and photogrammetry. After some years in the Royal Engineers and then more working in the IT industry, he decided to develop his lifelong interest in history, archaeology and architecture by working on commercial archaeological projects. In 2006 he founded Aerial-Cam, which combined his archaeological experience and extensive photography skills to provide a specialist service recording evidence via telescopic masts, kites and Remotely Piloted Aircraft.

The Stonehenge Riverside Project was the first of many research projects where Aerial-Cam was put to the test. Since then other projects, ranging from Orkney to Rapa Nui (Easter Island), have seen Adam constantly developing equipment and techniques to meet the challenges of excavation, building recording and landscape survey.

Suggested
further reading

Aronson, M, with Parker Pearson, M, 2010 *If Stones Could Speak: unlocking the secrets of Stonehenge*. Washington DC: National Geographic Society

Atkinson, R J C, 1956 *Stonehenge*. London: Hamish Hamilton

Bevins, R E, Ixer, R A and Pearce, N, 2014 Carn Goedog is the likely major source of Stonehenge doleritic bluestones: evidence based on compatible element discrimination and principal components analysis, *J Archaeol Sci*, **42**, 179–93

Bowden, M, Soutar, S, Field, D and Barber, M, 2015 *The Stonehenge Landscape: analysing the Stonehenge World Heritage Site*. London: Historic England

Cleal, R M J, Walker, K E and Montague, R, 1995 *Stonehenge in its Landscape: twentieth-century excavations*. London: English Heritage

Darvill, T C and Wainwright, G J, 2009 Stonehenge excavations 2008, *Antiq J*, **89**, 1–19

Darvill, T C, Marshall, P, Parker Pearson, M and Wainwright, G J, 2012 Stonehenge remodelled, *Antiquity*, **86**, 1021–40

Gaffney, V, 2014 New light on Stonehenge, *Current Archaeology*, **296** http://www.archaeology.co.uk/issues/ca-296-on-sale-now.htm

Ixer, R A and Bevins, R E, 2011 Craig Rhos-y-felin, Pont Saeson is the dominant source of the Stonehenge rhyolitic 'debitage', *Archaeology in Wales*, **50**, 21–32

Larsson, M and Parker Pearson, M (eds), 2007 *From Stonehenge to the Baltic: cultural diversity in the third millennium BC*. BAR Internat Ser **1692**. Oxford: British Archaeological Reports

Parker Pearson, M, 2012 *Stonehenge: exploring the greatest Stone Age mystery*. London: Simon & Schuster

Parker Pearson, M and Ramilisonina, 1998 Stonehenge for the ancestors: the stones pass on the message, *Antiquity,* **72**, 308–26

Parker Pearson, M, Chamberlain, A, Jay, M, Marshall, P, Pollard, J, Richards, C, Thomas, J, Tilley, C and Welham, K, 2009 Who was buried at Stonehenge?, *Antiquity*, **83**, 23–39

Pitts, M W, 2001 *Hengeworld*. 2nd edn. London: Arrow Books

Pitts, M W, 2014 The new face of Stonehenge, *British Archaeology*, **137**. http://www.britisharchaeology.org/ba137

Richards, J, 2007 *Stonehenge: the story so far*. London: English Heritage

Ruggles, C, 1997 Astronomy and Stonehenge, in B Cunliffe and C Renfrew (eds) *Science and Stonehenge*. London: British Academy and Oxford University Press, 203–29

Bibliography

Albarella, U and Serjeantson, D, 2002 A passion for pork: meat consumption at the British Late Neolithic site of Durrington Walls, in P Miracle and N Milner (eds) *Consuming Passions and Patterns of Consumption*. Cambridge: Cambridge University Press, 33–49

Allen, M J, 1997 Environment and land-use: the economic development of the communities who built Stonehenge (an economy to support the stone), in Cunliffe and Renfrew (eds), 115–44

Allen, M J and Gardiner, J, 2002 A sense of time: cultural markers in the Mesolithic of southern England, in B David and M Wilson (eds) *Inscribed Landscapes: marking and making places*. Honolulu: University of Hawai'i Press, 139–53

Allen, M J, Gardiner, J and Sheridan, A (eds), 2012 *Is there a British Chalcolithic?: people, place and polity in the later 3rd millennium*. Prehist Soc Res Paper **4**. Oxford: Oxbow

Annable, F K and Simpson, D D A, 1964 *Guide Catalogue of the Neolithic and Bronze Age Collections in Devizes Museum*. Devizes: Wiltshire Archaeological and Natural History Society

Aronson, M, with Parker Pearson, M, 2010 *If Stones Could Speak: unlocking the secrets of Stonehenge*. Washington DC: National Geographic Society

Ashbee, P, 1993 The Medway megaliths in perspective, *Archaeologia Cantiana*, **111**, 57–111

Ashbee, P, 1998 Stonehenge: its possible non-completion, slighting and dilapidation, *Wiltshire Archaeol Natur Hist Mag*, **91**, 139–42

Ashmore, P J, 1996 *Neolithic and Bronze Age Scotland*. London: Batsford/Historic Scotland

Atkinson, R J C, 1956 *Stonehenge*. London: Hamish Hamilton

Atkinson, R J C, 1979 *Stonehenge*. 3rd edn. Harmondsworth: Penguin

Atkinson, R J C, Piggott, C M and Sandars, N, 1951 *Excavations at Dorchester, Oxon*. Oxford: Ashmolean Museum

Barclay, A J and Halpin, C, 1998 *Excavations at Barrow Hills, Radley, Oxfordshire. Volume I: The Neolithic and Bronze Age monument complex*. Oxford: Oxford Archaeological Unit

Barclay, A J and Harding, J (eds), 1999 *Pathways and Ceremonies: the cursus monuments of Britain and Ireland*. Oxford: Oxbow

Barclay, A J, Beacan, N, Bradley, P, Chaffey, G, Challinor, D, McKinley, J I, Powell, A and Marshall, P, 2009 New evidence for mid-late Neolithic burial from the Colne valley, west London, *Past*, **63**, 4–6

Barclay, A J, Gray, M and Lambrick, G, 1995 *Excavations at the Devil's Quoits, Stanton Harcourt, Oxfordshire, 1972–73 and 1988*. Oxford: Oxford Archaeology

Barclay, G J and Russell-White, C, 1993 Excavations in the ceremonial complex of the fourth to second millennium BC at Balfarg/Balbirnie, Glenrothes, Fife, *Proc Soc Antiq Scotl*, **123**, 43–210

Barker, C T, 1992 *The Chambered Tombs of South-west Wales: a re-assessment of the Neolithic burial monuments of Carmarthenshire and Pembrokeshire*. Oxford: Oxbow

Barker, G, 2009 *The Agricultural Revolution in Prehistory: why did foragers become farmers?* Oxford: Oxford University Press

Barrett, J and Fewster, K, 1998 Is the medium the message?, *Antiquity*, **72**, 847–51

Barrett, J C, Bradley, R and Green, M, 1991 *Landscape, Monuments and Society: the prehistory of Cranborne Chase*. Cambridge: Cambridge University Press

BBC, 2010 Archaeologists unearth Neolithic henge at Stonehenge, http://www.bbc.co.uk/news/uk-england-10718522

Bell, M and Walker, M J C, 1992 *Late Quaternary Environmental Change: physical and human perspectives*. Harlow: Longman

Bender, B, 1998 *Stonehenge: making space*. London: Berg

Bevins, R E, Ixer, R A and Pearce, N, 2014 Carn Goedog is the likely major source of Stonehenge doleritic bluestones: evidence based on compatible element discrimination and principal components analysis, *J Archaeol Sci*, **42**, 179–93

Booth, A St J and Stone, J F S, 1952 A trial flint mine at Durrington, Wiltshire, *Wiltshire Archaeol Natur Hist Mag*, **54**, 381–8

Bowden, M, Soutar, S, Field, D and Barber, M, 2015 *The Stonehenge Landscape: analysing the Stonehenge World Heritage Site*. London: Historic England

Bowen, H C and Smith, I F, 1977 Sarsen stones in Wessex: the Society's first investigations in the Evolution of the Landscape Project, *Antiq J*, **57**, 185–96

Bradley, R, 1975 Maumbury Rings, Dorchester: the excavations of 1908–1913, *Archaeologia*, **105**, 1–98

Bradley, R, 1993 *Altering the Earth*. Edinburgh: Society of Antiquaries of Scotland

Bradley, R, 2000a *The Archaeology of Natural Places*. London: Routledge

Bradley, R, 2000b *The Good Stones: a new investigation of the Clava Cairns*. Edinburgh: Society of Antiquaries of Scotland

Bradley, R, 2005 *The Moon and the Bonfire: an investigation of three stone circles in north-east Scotland*. Edinburgh: Society of Antiquaries of Scotland

Bradley, R, 2012 *The Idea of Order: the circular archetype in prehistory*. London: Routledge

Bradley, R and Chambers, R, 1988 A new study of the cursus complex at Dorchester-on-Thames, *Oxford J Archaeol*, **7**, 271–89

Bradley, R and Edmonds, M, 1993 *Interpreting the Axe Trade: production and exchange in Neolithic Britain*. Cambridge: Cambridge University Press

Brindley, A, 1999 Sequence and dating in the Grooved Ware tradition, in Cleal and MacSween (eds), 133–44

Britnell, W, 1982 The excavation of two round barrows at Trelystan, Powys, *Proc Prehist Soc*, **48**, 133–201

Brodie, N, 1994 *The Neolithic–Bronze Age Transition in Britain*. BAR Brit Ser **238**. Oxford: British Archaeological Reports

Brophy, K, 2000 Water coincidence? Cursus monuments and rivers, in A Ritchie (ed) *Neolithic Orkney in its European Context*. Oxford: Oxbow, 59–70

Brophy, K, 2007 From big houses to cult houses: Early Neolithic timber halls in Scotland, *Proc Prehist Soc*, **73**, 75–96

Burgess, C and Shennan, S, 1976 The Beaker phenomenon: some suggestions, in C Burgess and R Miket (eds) *Settlement and Economy in the Third and Second Millennia B.C.* BAR Brit Ser **33**. Oxford: British Archaeological Reports, 309–31

Burl, A, 1976 *The Stone Circles of the British Isles.* New Haven & London: Yale University Press

Burl, A, 1987 *The Stonehenge People.* London: J M Dent

Burl, A, 1993 *From Carnac to Callanish: the prehistoric stone rows and avenues of Britain, Ireland, and Brittany.* New Haven & London: Yale University Press

Burl, A, 2002 *Prehistoric Avebury.* 2nd edn. New Haven & London: Yale University Press

Burl, A, 2006 *Stonehenge: a new history of the world's greatest stone circle.* London: Constable

Burrow, S, 2010 The formative henge: speculations drawn from the circular traditions of Wales and adjacent counties, in J Leary, T Darvill and D Field (eds) *Round Mounds and Monumentality in the British Neolithic and Beyond.* Oxford: Oxbow, 182–96

Caesar, J [1951] *The Conquest of Gaul.* Trans by S A Handford. Harmondsworth: Penguin

Calado, M, 2002 Standing stones and natural outcrops: the role of ritual monuments in the Neolithic transition of the central Alentejo, in C Scarre (ed) *Monuments and Landscape in Atlantic Europe: perception and society during the Neolithic and Early Bronze Age.* London: Routledge, 17–35

Card, N, 2010 Neolithic temples of the Northern Isles, *Current Archaeology*, **241**, 12–19

Case, H, 2004 Beakers and the Beaker culture, in J Czebreszuk (ed) *Similar but Different: Bell Beakers in Europe.* Poznan: Adam Mickiewicz University, 11–34

Cassen, S, 2009 *Exercice de Stèle: une archéologie des pierres dressées, refléxion autour des menhirs de Carnac.* Paris: Errance

Cassen, S, Lanos, P, Dufresne, P, Oberlin, C, Delqué-Kolic, E and Le Goffic, M, 2009 Datations sur site (Table des Marchands, alignement du Grand Menhir, Er Grah) et modélisation chronologique du Néolithique morbihannais, in S Cassen (ed) *Autour de la Table: explorations archéologiques et discours savants sur des architectures néolithiques à Locmariaquer, Morbihan (Table des Marchands et Grand Menhir).* Nantes: Université de Nantes, 737–68

Chamberlain, A and Parker Pearson, M, 2007 Units of measurement in Late Neolithic southern Britain, in Larsson and Parker Pearson (eds), 169–74

Chapman, H, Hewson, M and Wilkes, M, 2010. The Catholme ceremonial complex, Staffordshire, UK, *Proc Prehist Soc*, **76**, 135–63

Childe, V G, 1931 *Skara Brae: a Pictish village in Orkney.* London: Kegan Paul

Chippindale, C, 1994 *Stonehenge Complete.* Revised edn. London: Thames & Hudson

Christie, P M, 1963 The Stonehenge Cursus, *Wiltshire Archaeol Natur Hist Mag*, **58**, 370–82

Christie, P M, 1967 A barrow cemetery of the second millennium BC in Wiltshire, England, *Proc Prehist Soc*, **33**, 336–66

Clarke, D L, 1976 *Beaker Pottery of Great Britain and Ireland.* Cambridge: Cambridge University Press

Cleal, R M J and Allen, M J, 1994 Investigation of tree-damaged barrows on King Barrow Ridge and Luxenborough Plantation, Amesbury, *Wiltshire Archaeol Natur Hist Mag*, **87**, 54–84

Cleal, R M J and MacSween, A (eds), 1999 *Grooved Ware in Great Britain and Ireland*. Oxford: Oxbow

Cleal, R M J, Allen, M and Newman, C, 2004 An archaeological and environmental study of the Neolithic and later prehistoric landscape of the Avon valley and Durrington Walls environs, *Wiltshire Archaeol Natur Hist Mag*, **97**, 218–48

Cleal, R M J, Walker, K E and Montague, R, 1995 *Stonehenge in its Landscape: twentieth-century excavations*. London: English Heritage

Clough, T and Cummins, W A (eds), 1979 *Stone Axe Studies: archaeological, petrological, experimental and ethnographic*. CBA Research Report **23**. London: Council for British Archaeology

Collard, M, Edinborough, K, Shennan, S J, and Thomas, M G, 2009 Radiocarbon evidence indicates that migrants introduced farming to Britain, *J Archaeol Sci*, **37**(4), 866–70

Colt Hoare, R, 1812 *The Ancient History of South Wiltshire*. London: William Miller

Cowie, T and MacSween, A, 1999 Grooved Ware from Scotland: a review, in Cleal and MacSween (eds), 48–56

Crawford, O G S, 1924 The Stonehenge Avenue, *Antiq J*, **4**, 57–8

Crowley, D A, Pugh, R B and Stevenson, J H, 1995 *A History of Amesbury, Bulford and Durrington*. Trowbridge: Wiltshire County Council

Cummings, V and Whittle, A W R, 2004 *Places of Special Virtue: megaliths in the Neolithic landscapes of Wales*. Oxford: Oxbow

Cummins, W A, 1979 Neolithic stone axes: distribution and trade in England and Wales, in Clough and Cummins (eds), 5–12

Cunliffe, B and Renfrew, C (eds), 1997 *Science and Stonehenge*. London: British Academy and Oxford University Press

Cunnington, B H, 1924 The 'blue stone' from Boles Barrow. *Wiltshire Archaeol Natur Hist Mag*, **42**, 431–7

Cunnington, M E, 1929 *Woodhenge*. Devizes: Simpson

Cunnington, M E, 1931 The Sanctuary on Overton Hill near Avebury, *Wiltshire Archaeol Natur Hist Mag*, **45**, 300–35

Curtis, N and Wilkin, N, 2012 The regionality of Beakers and bodies in the Chalcolithic of north-east Scotland, in Allen, Gardiner and Sheridan (eds), 237–56

Danaher, E, 2007 *Monumental Beginnings: the archaeology of the N4 Sligo Inner Relief Road*. Dublin: National Roads Authority

Daniel, G, 1958 *The Megalith Builders of Western Europe*. London: Hutchinson

Darvill, T C, 2005 *Stonehenge World Heritage Site: an archaeological research framework*. London & Bournemouth: English Heritage & Bournemouth University

Darvill, T C, 2006 *Stonehenge: the biography of a landscape*. Stroud: Tempus

Darvill, T C, 2007 Towards the within: Stonehenge and its purpose, in D A Barrowclough and C Malone (eds) *Cult in Context: reconsidering ritual in archaeology*. Oxford: Oxbow, 148–57

Darvill, T C, 2010 *Prehistoric Britain*. 2nd edn. London: Routledge, 77–187

Darvill, T C and Wainwright, G J, 2002 Strumble–Preseli Ancient Communities and Environment Study (SPACES): first report 2002, *Archaeology in Wales*, **42**, 17–28

Darvill, T C and Wainwright, G J, 2003 Stone circles, oval settings and henges in south-west Wales and beyond, *Antiq J*, **83**, 9–45

Darvill, T C and Wainwright, G J, 2009 Stonehenge excavations 2008, *Antiq J*, **89**, 1–19

Darvill, T C, Lüth, F, Rassmann, K, Fischer, A and Winkelmann, K, 2012 Stonehenge, Wiltshire, UK: high resolution geophysical surveys in the surrounding landscape, 2011, *European J Archaeol*, **16**, 63–93

Darvill, T C, Marshall, P, Parker Pearson, M and Wainwright, G J, 2012 Stonehenge remodelled, *Antiquity*, **86**, 1021–40

Darvill, T C, Morgan Evans, D and Wainwright, G J, 2003 Strumble–Preseli Ancient Communities and Environment Study (SPACES): second report 2003, *Archaeology in Wales*, **43**, 3–12

Darvill, T C, Morgan Evans, D and Wainwright, G J, 2004 Strumble–Preseli Ancient Communities and Environment Study (SPACES): third report 2004, *Archaeology in Wales*, **44**, 104–9

Darvill, T C, Morgan Evans, D, Fyfe, R and Wainwright, G J, 2005 Strumble–Preseli Ancient Communities and Environment Study (SPACES): fourth report 2005, *Archaeology in Wales*, **45**, 17–23

Darwin, C, 1881 *The Formation of Vegetable Mould Through the Action of Worms, with observations on their habits.* London: John Murray

David, A, Cole, M, Horsley, T, Linford, N, Linford, P and Martin, L, 2004 A rival to Stonehenge? Geophysical survey at Stanton Drew, England, *Antiquity*, **78**, 341–58

Dehn, T and Hansen, S I, 2006 Birch bark in Danish passage tombs, *J Danish Archaeol*, **14**, 23–44

Dixon, P, 1988 The Neolithic settlements on Crickley Hill, in C Burgess, P Topping, C Mordant and M Madison (eds) *Enclosures and Defences in the Neolithic of Western Europe.* BAR Internat Ser **403**. Oxford: British Archaeological Reports, 75–88

Durrani, N, 2009 First written reference to soul, *Current World Archaeology*, **33**, 12

Entwistle, R and Grant, A, 1989 The evidence for cereal cultivation and animal husbandry in the southern British Neolithic and Bronze Age, in A Milles, D Williams and N Gardner (eds) *The Beginnings of Agriculture.* BAR Internat Ser **496**. Oxford: British Archaeological Reports, 203–15

Eogan, G, 1986 *Knowth and the Passage-Tombs of Ireland.* London: Thames and Hudson

Eogan, G and Roche, H, 1997 *Excavations at Knowth. Volume 2.* Dublin: Royal Irish Academy

Evans, J A, Chenery, C and Fitzpatrick, A P, 2006 Bronze Age childhood migration of individuals near Stonehenge, revealed by strontium and oxygen isotope tooth enamel analysis, *Archaeometry*, **48**, 309–21

Evans, J G, 1984 Stonehenge – the environment in the Late Neolithic and Early Bronze Age and a Beaker-Age burial. *Wiltshire Archaeol Natur Hist Mag*, **78**, 7–30

Farrer, P, 1918 Durrington Walls, or Long Walls. *Wiltshire Archaeol Natur Hist Mag*, **40**, 95–103

Fenwick, J, 1995 The manufacture of the decorated macehead from Knowth, County Meath, *J Royal Soc Antiq Ireland*, **125**, 51–60

Field, D and Pearson, T, 2010 *Stonehenge World Heritage Site landscape project. Stonehenge, Amesbury, Wiltshire. Archaeological Survey Report.* London: English Heritage

Field, D, Pearson, T, Barber, M and Payne, A, 2010 Introducing 'Stonehedge' (and other curious earthworks), *British Archaeology*, **111**, 32–5

Fitzpatrick, A P, 2002 'The Amesbury Archer': a well-furnished Early Bronze Age burial in southern England, *Antiquity*, **76**, 629–30

Fitzpatrick, A P, 2011 *The Amesbury Archer and the Boscombe Bowmen: Bell Beaker burials at Boscombe Down, Amesbury, Wiltshire*. Oxford: Oxbow

Flinders Petrie, W M, 1880 *Stonehenge: plans, description, and theories*. London: Edward Stanford

French, C A I, Scaife, R and Allen, M J, 2012 Durrington Walls to West Amesbury by way of Stonehenge: a major transformation of the Holocene landscape, *Antiq J*, **92**, 1–36

Gaffney, V, 2014 New light on Stonehenge, *Current Archaeology*, **296** http://www.archaeology.co.uk/issues/ca-296-on-sale-now.htm

Garwood, P, 1999 Grooved Ware in southern Britain. Chronology and interpretation, in Cleal and MacSween (eds), 145–76

Gibson, A M, 1992 The timber circle at Sarn-y-Bryn-Caled, Welshpool, Powys: ritual and sacrifice in Bronze Age mid-Wales, *Antiquity*, **66**, 84–92

Gibson, A M, 1998a Hindwell and the Neolithic palisaded sites of Britain and Ireland, in A Gibson and D D A Simpson (eds) *Prehistoric Ritual and Religion: essays in honour of Aubrey Burl*. Stroud: Sutton, 68–79

Gibson, A M, 1998b *Stonehenge and Timber Circles*. Stroud: Tempus

Gibson, A M, 1999 *The Walton Basin project: excavation and survey in a prehistoric landscape 1993–97*. CBA Research Report **118**. York: Council for British Archaeology

Gibson, A M, 2007 A Beaker veneer? Some evidence from the burial record, in Larsson and Parker Pearson (eds), 47–64

Gibson, A M, 2008 Were henges ghost-traps?, *Current Archaeology*, **214**, 34–9

Gibson, A M, 2010 Dating Balbirnie: recent radiocarbon dates from the stone circle and cairn at Balbirnie, Fife, and a review of its place in the overall Balfarg/Balbirnie site sequence, *Proc Soc Antiq Scotl*, **140**, 51–77

Gibson, A M and Bayliss, A, 2009 Recent research at Duggleby Howe, North Yorkshire, *Archaeol J*, **166**, 39–78

Gillings, M and Pollard, J M, 2004 *Avebury*. London: Duckworth.

Gillings, M, Pollard, J, Wheatley, D and Peterson, R, 2008 *Landscape of the Megaliths: excavation and fieldwork on the Avebury monuments, 1997–2003*. Oxford: Oxbow

Giot, P-R, 1987 *Barnenez, Carn, Guennoc*. Rennes: Laboratoire d'Anthropologie, Préhistoire, Protohistoire et Quaternaire Armoricains

Gowland, W, 1902 Recent excavations at Stonehenge, *Archaeologia*, **58**, 37–105

Green, C P, 1973 Pleistocene river gravels and the Stonehenge problem, *Nature*, **243**, 214–16

Green, M, 2000 *A Landscape Revealed: 10,000 years on a chalkland farm*. Stroud: Tempus

Grimes, W F, 1936 The megalithic monuments of Wales, *Proc Prehist Soc*, **2**, 106–39

Grimes, W F, 1949 Pentre-ifan burial chamber, Pembrokeshire, *Archaeol Cambrensis*, **100**, 3–23

Grimes, W F, 1963 The stone circles and related monuments of Wales, in I Foster and L Alcock (eds) *Culture and Environment: essays in honour of Sir Cyril Fox*. London: Routledge & Kegan Paul, 93–152

Haak, W, Forster, P, Bramanti, B, Matsumura, S, Brandt, G, Tänzer, M, Villems, R, Renfrew, C, Gronenborn, D, Alt, K W and Burger, J, 2005 Ancient DNA from the first European farmers in 7500-year-old Neolithic sites, *Science*, **310**, 1016–18

Harding, J, 2003 *Henge Monuments of the British Isles*. Stroud: Tempus

Harding, P, 1988 The chalk plaque pit, Amesbury, *Proc Prehist Soc*, **54**, 320–7

Hardy, F, 1928 *The Early Life of Thomas Hardy, 1840–91*. London: Macmillan

Harrison, R J, 1980 *The Beaker Folk*. London: Thames & Hudson

Harrison, R J and Martín, A M, 2001 Bell Beakers and social complexity in central Spain, in Nicolis (ed), 111–24

Hawkins, G S, with White, J B, 1965 *Stonehenge Decoded*. Garden City NY: Doubleday

Hawley, W, 1921 The excavations at Stonehenge, *Antiq J*, **1**, 19–39

Hawley, W, 1922 Second report on the excavations at Stonehenge, *Antiq J*, **2**, 36–51

Hawley, W, 1923 Third report on the excavations at Stonehenge, *Antiq J*, **3**, 13–20

Hawley, W, 1924 Fourth report on the excavations at Stonehenge, *Antiq J*, **4**, 30–9

Hawley, W, 1925 Report of the excavations at Stonehenge during the season of 1923, *Antiq J*, **5**, 21–50

Hawley, W, 1926 Report on the excavations at Stonehenge during the season of 1924, *Antiq J*, **6**, 1–25

Hawley, W, 1928 Report on the excavations at Stonehenge during 1925 and 1926, *Antiq J*, **8**, 149–76

Healy, F, 1997 Site 3. Flagstones, in R J C Smith, F Healy, M J Allen, E L Morris, I Barnes and P J Woodward *Excavations along the Route of the Dorchester By-pass, Dorset, 1986–8* (Report No 11). Salisbury: Wessex Archaeology, 27–48

Healy, F, 2008 Causewayed enclosures and the Early Neolithic: the chronology and character of monument building and settlement in Kent, Surrey and Sussex in the early to mid-4th millennium cal BC, *South East Research Framework Resource Assessment*. 1–29. https://shareweb.kent.gov.uk/Documents/Leisure_ and_Culture/Heritage/frances-healy.pdf

Healy, F, 2012 Chronology, corpses, ceramics, copper and lithics, in Allen, Gardiner and Sheridan (eds), 144–63

Henry of Huntingdon, 1129–1154 [1991] *Historia Anglorum*. Felinfach: Llanerch Press

Hey, G, Garwood, P, Robinson, M, Barclay, A and Bradley, P, 2011 *The Thames Through Time: the archaeology of the gravel terraces of the middle and upper Thames. Early prehistory to 1500 BC. Part 2 – The Mesolithic, Neolithic and Early Bronze Age and the establishment of permanent human occupation in the valley.* Oxford: Oxford Archaeology

Hill, J, 2008 The secret measurement of Stonehenge. http://www.johnhillma.co.uk/press_release.php

Hill, P, 1961 Sarsen stones of Stonehenge, *Science*, **133**, 1216–22

Hodder, I, 1994 Architecture and meaning: the example of Neolithic houses and tombs, in M Parker Pearson and C Richards (eds) *Architecture and Order: approaches to social space*. London: Routledge, 73–86

Hoskins, J, 1986 So my name shall live: stone-dragging and grave-building in Kodi, West Sumba, *Bijdragen tot de Taal-, Land- en Volkenkunde*, **142**, 31–51

Hoyle, F, 1977 *On Stonehenge*. San Francisco: W H Freeman

Hunter-Mann, K, 1999 Excavations at Vespasian's Camp Iron Age hillfort, 1987, *Wiltshire Archaeol Natur Hist Mag*, **92**, 39–52

Ixer, R A and Bevins, R E, 2011a Craig Rhos-y-felin, Pont Saeson is the dominant source of the Stonehenge rhyolitic 'debitage', *Archaeology in Wales*, **50**, 21–32

Ixer, R A and Bevins, R E, 2011b The detailed petrography of six orthostats from the bluestone circle, Stonehenge, *Wiltshire Archaeol Natur Hist Mag*, **104**, 1–14

Ixer, R A and Turner, P, 2006 A detailed re-examination of the petrography of the Altar Stone and other non-sarsen sandstones from Stonehenge as a guide to their provenance, *Wiltshire Archaeol Natur Hist Mag*, **99**, 1–9

Jacques, D, 2010 Amesbury excavation: summary of AA309 students' field work at Vespasian's Camp, near Stonehenge, Wiltshire, 2005–2009. http://www.open.ac.uk/Arts/classical-studies/amesbury/index.shtml

Jacques, D, Phillips, T and Lyons, T, 2012 Vespasian's Camp: cradle of Stonehenge?, *Current Archaeology*, **271**, 28–33

Jay, M and Richards, M, 2007 The Beaker People Project: progress and prospects for the carbon, nitrogen and sulphur isotope analysis of collagen, in Larsson and Parker Pearson (eds), 77–82

Jay, M, Parker Pearson, M, Richards, M P, Nehlich, O, Montgomery, J, Chamberlain, A and Sheridan, A, 2011 The Beaker People Project: an interim report on the progress of the isotopic analysis of the organic skeletal material, in Allen, Gardiner and Sheridan (eds), 226–36

Johnson, A, 2008 *Solving Stonehenge: the new key to an ancient enigma*. London: Thames & Hudson

Jones, G and Rowley-Conwy, P, 2007 On the importance of cereal cultivation in the British Neolithic, in S Colledge and J Conolly (eds) *The Origins and Spread of Domestic Plants in Southwest Asia and Europe*. Walnut Creek CA: Left Coast Press, 391–419

Jones, I, 1655 *The Most Notable Antiquity of Great Britain, vulgarly called Stone-Heng*. London: Daniel Pakeman

Kinnes, I, 1979 *Round Barrows and Ring-ditches in the British Neolithic*. British Museum Occasional Paper **7**. London: British Museum Press

Kinnes, I A, Schadla-Hall, T, Chadwick, P and Dean, P, 1983 Duggleby Howe reconsidered, *Archaeol J*, **140**, 83–108

Large, J-M and Mens, E, 2008 L'alignment du Douet à Hoedic (Morbihan, France), *L'Anthropologie*, **112**, 544–71

Large, J-M and Mens, E, 2009 The Douet alignment on the island of Hoedic (Morbihan): new insights into standing stone alignments in Brittany, *Oxford J Archaeol*, **28**, 239–54

Larson, G, Albarella, U, Dobney, K, Rowley-Conwy, P, Schibler, J, Tresset, A, Vigne, J D, Edwards, C J, Schlumbaum, A, Dinu, A, Balaçsescu, A, Dolman, G, Tagliacozzo, A, Manaseryan, N, Miracle, P, Van Wijngaarden-Bakker, L, Masseti, M, Bradley, D G and Cooper, A, 2007, Ancient DNA, pig domestication, and the spread of the Neolithic into Europe, *Proc Nat Acad Sciences*, **104**(39), 15276–81

Larsson, M and Parker Pearson, M (eds), 2007 *From Stonehenge to the Baltic: cultural diversity in the third millennium BC*. BAR Internat Ser **1692**. Oxford: British Archaeological Reports

Lawson, A J, 2007 *Chalkland: an archaeology of Stonehenge and its region*. Salisbury: Hobnob Press

Leary, J and Field, D, 2010 *The Story of Silbury Hill*. London: English Heritage

Leary, J and Marshall, P, 2012 The giants of Wessex: the chronology of the three largest mounds in Wiltshire, UK, *Antiquity*, **86**. http://antiquity.ac.uk/projgall/leary334/

Leary, J, Field, D and Russell, M, 2010 Marvels at Marden henge, *Past*, **66**, 13–14

Leivers, M and Moore, C, 2008 *Archaeology on the A303 Stonehenge Improvement*. Salisbury: Wessex Archaeology

Lewis, J and Mullin, D, 2010 Dating the Priddy Circles, Somerset, *Past*, **64**, 4–5

Longworth, I H and Cleal, R M J, 1999 Grooved Ware gazetteer, in Cleal and MacSween (eds), 177–206

Lynch, F, 1975 Excavations at Carreg Samson, Mathry, Pembrokeshire, *Archaeol Cambrensis*, **124**, 15–35

Lynch, F and Musson, C, 2004 A prehistoric and early medieval complex at Llandegai, near Bangor, north Wales, *Archaeol Cambrensis*, **150**, 17–142

Márquez-Romero, J E and Fernández Ruiz, J, 2009 *The Dolmens of Antequera: official guide to the archaeological complex*. Malaga: Junta de Andalucía, Consejería de Cultura

McKinley, J I, 1994 Bone fragment size in British cremation burials and its implications for pyre technology and ritual, *J Archaeol Sci*, **21**, 339–42

McKinley, J I, 1997 Bronze Age 'barrows' and the funerary rites and rituals of cremation, *Proc Prehist Soc*, **63**, 129–45

Mercer, R (ed), 1977 *Beakers in Britain and Europe*. BAR Internat Ser **331**. Oxford: British Archaeological Reports

Mercer, R, 1999 The origins of warfare in the British Isles, in J Carman and A Harding (eds) *Ancient Warfare: archaeological perspectives*. Stroud: Sutton, 143–56

Mercer, R and Healy, F, 2008 *Hambledon Hill, Dorset, England: excavation and survey of a Neolithic monument complex and its surrounding landscape*. 2 vols. London: English Heritage

Metcalf, P and Huntington, R, 1991 *Celebrations of Death: the anthropology of mortuary ritual*. Cambridge: Cambridge University Press

Michell, J, 1981 *Ancient Metrology*. Bristol: Pentacle Books

Mitchell, G F, 1992 Notes on some non-local cobbles at the entrance to the passage-graves at Newgrange and Knowth, County Meath, *J Roy Soc Antiq Irel*, **122**, 128–45

Montgomery, J, Budd, P and Evans, J, 2000 Reconstructing the lifetime movements of ancient people: a Neolithic case study from southern England, *European J Archaeol*, **3**, 407–22

Montgomery, J, Cooper, R and Evans, J, 2007 Foragers, farmers or foreigners? An assessment of dietary strontium isotope variation in Middle Neolithic and Early Bronze Age East Yorkshire, in Larsson and Parker Pearson (eds), 65–75

Morgan, C L, 1887 The stones of Stanton Drew: their source and origin, *Proc Somerset Archaeol Natur Hist Soc*, **33**, 37–50

Mortimer, J R, 1905 *Fifty Years' Researches in British and Saxon Burial Mounds of East Yorkshire*. London: A Brown & Sons

Mukherjee, A J, 2004 The importance of pigs in the Later British Neolithic: integrating stable isotope evidence from lipid residues in archaeological potsherds, animal bone, and modern animal tissues. Unpublished PhD thesis, University of Bristol

Mukherjee, A J, Gibson, A M and Evershed, R P, 2008 Trends in pig product processing at British Neolithic Grooved Ware sites traced through organic residues in potsherds, *J Archaeol Sci*, **35**, 2059–73

Müller, J and van Willigen, S, 2001 New radiocarbon evidence for European Bell Beakers and the consequences for the diffusion of the Bell Beaker phenomenon, in Nicolis (ed), 59–80

Neal, J, 2000 *All Done with Mirrors*. London: The Secret Academy

Needham, S, 2005 Transforming Beaker culture in north-west Europe: processes of fusion and fission, *Proc Prehist Soc*, **71**, 171–217

Needham, S, Lawson, A J and Woodward, A, 2010 'A noble group of barrows': Bush Barrow and the Normanton Down Early Bronze Age cemetery two centuries on, *Antiq J*, **90**, 1–39

Needham, S, Parker Pearson, M, Tyler, A, Richards, M and Jay, M, 2010 A first 'Wessex I' date from Wessex, *Antiquity*, **84**, 363–73

Nicolis, F (ed), 2001 *Bell Beakers Today: pottery, people, culture, symbols in prehistoric Europe*. Proceedings of the International Colloquium at Riva del Garda 11–16 May 1998. Trento: Servicio Beni Culturali, Provincia Autonoma di Trento (2 vols)

Noble, G, 2006 *Neolithic Scotland: timber, stone, earth and fire*. Edinburgh: Edinburgh University Press

Noble, G and Brophy, K, 2011 Ritual and remembrance at a prehistoric ceremonial complex in central Scotland: excavations at Forteviot, Perth and Kinross, *Antiquity*, **85**, 787–804

North, J, 1996 *Stonehenge: Neolithic man and the cosmos*. London: Harper Collins

O'Kelly, M J, 1994 *Newgrange: archaeology, art and legend*. 2nd edn. London: Thames & Hudson

O'Kelly, M J and O'Kelly, C, 1983 The tumulus of Dowth, County Meath, *Proc Roy Irish Acad C* **78**, 249–352

Oswald, A, 1969 Excavations at Barford, Warwickshire, *Trans Birmingham Warwickshire Archaeol Soc*, **83**, 3–54

Oswald, A C, Dyer, C and Barber, M, 2001 *The Creation of Monuments: Neolithic causewayed enclosures in the British Isles*. Swindon: English Heritage

Parker Pearson, M, 1999 The Earlier Bronze Age, in J Hunter and I Ralston (eds) *The Archaeology of Britain: an introduction from the Palaeolithic to the Industrial Revolution*. London: Routledge, 77–94

Parker Pearson, M, 2003 Food, culture and identity in the Neolithic and Early Bronze Age: an introduction and overview, in M Parker Pearson (ed) *Food, Identity and Culture in the Neolithic and Early Bronze Age*. BAR Internat Ser **1117**. Oxford: British Archaeological Reports, 1–30

Parker Pearson, M, 2005 *Bronze Age Britain*. London: Batsford & English Heritage

Parker Pearson, M, 2006 The Beaker People Project: mobility and diet in the British Early Bronze Age, *The Archaeologist*, **61**, 14–15

Parker Pearson, M, 2007 The Stonehenge Riverside Project: excavations at the east entrance of Durrington Walls, in Larsson and Parker Pearson (eds), 125–44

Parker Pearson, M, 2008 When did copper first come to Britain?, *British Archaeology*, **101**, 25

Parker Pearson, M, 2012 *Stonehenge: exploring the greatest Stone Age mystery*. London: Simon & Schuster

Parker Pearson, M and Ramilisonina, 1998a Stonehenge for the ancestors: the stones pass on the message, *Antiquity*, **72**, 308–26

Parker Pearson, M and Ramilisonina, 1998b Stonehenge for the ancestors: part two, *Antiquity*, **72**, 855–6

Parker Pearson, M and Richards, C, 1994 Architecture and order: spatial representation and archaeology, in M Parker Pearson and C Richards (eds) *Architecture and Order: approaches to social space*. London: Routledge, 38–72

Parker Pearson, M, Chamberlain, A, Jay, M, Marshall, P, Pollard, J, Richards, C, Thomas, J, Tilley, C and Welham, K, 2009 Who was buried at Stonehenge?, *Antiquity*, **83**, 23–39

Parker Pearson, M, Cleal, R, Marshall, P, Needham, S, Pollard, J, Richards, C, Ruggles, C, Sheridan, A, Thomas, J, Tilley, C, Welham, K, Chamberlain, A, Chenery, C, Evans, J, Knüsel, C, Linford N, Martin, L, Montgomery, J, Payne, A and Richards, M, 2007 The age of Stonehenge, *Antiquity*, **81**, 617–39

Parker Pearson, M, with Godden, K, Heurtebize, G, Radimilahy, C, Ramilisonina, Retsihisatse, Schwenninger, J-L and Smith, H, 2010 *Pastoralists, Warriors and Colonists: the archaeology of southern Madagascar*. BAR Internat Ser **2139**. Oxford: British Archaeological Reports

Parker Pearson, M, Richards, M, Chamberlain, A, Evans, J and Jay, M (eds), forthcoming, *The Beaker People: isotopes, mobility and diet in prehistoric Britain*. Prehistoric Society monograph. Oxford: Oxbow

Passmore, A D, 1942 A disc barrow containing curious flints near Stonehenge, *Wiltshire Archaeol Nat Hist Mag*, **49**, 238

Petersen, F, 1972 Traditions of multiple burial in later Neolithic and Early Bronze Age Britain, *Archaeol J*, **129**, 22–55

Phillips, C W, 1936 The excavation of the Giants' Hills long barrow, Skendleby, Lincolnshire, *Archaeologia*, **85**, 37–106

Piggott, S, 1938 The Early Bronze Age in Wessex, *Proc Prehist Soc*, **4**, 52–106

Piggott, S, 1948a Destroyed megaliths in north Wiltshire, *Wiltshire Archaeol Nat Hist Mag*, **52**, 390–2

Piggott, S, 1948b The excavations at Cairnpapple Hill, West Lothian, 1947–8, *Proc Soc Antiq Scotl*, **82**, 68–123

Piggott, S, 1962 *The West Kennet Long Barrow*. London: HMSO

Piggott, S, 1968 *The Druids*. London: Pelican

Piggott, S, 1985 *William Stukeley: an eighteenth-century antiquary*. London: Thames & Hudson

Pipes, G, 2004 A new and unique theory on the movement of heavy stones. http://www.world-mysteries.com/gw_gpipes.htm

Pitts, M W, 1982 On the road to Stonehenge: report on the investigations beside the A344 in 1968, 1979 and 1980, *Proc Prehist Soc*, **48**, 75–132

Pitts, M W, 2001 *Hengeworld*. 2nd edn. London: Arrow Books

Pitts, M W, 2008 The big dig: Stonehenge. *British Archaeology*, **102**, 12–17

Pitts, M W, 2014 The new face of Stonehenge, *British Archaeology*, **137**. http://www.britisharchaeology.org/ba137

Pitts, M W, Bayliss, A, McKinley, J, Budd, P, Evans, J, Chenery, C, Reynolds, A and Semple, S, 2002 An Anglo-Saxon decapitation and burial from Stonehenge, *Wiltshire Archaeol Nat Hist Mag*, **95**, 131–46

Pollard, J, 1995a Inscribing space: formal deposition at the later Neolithic monument of Woodhenge, Wiltshire, *Proc Prehist Soc*, **61**, 137–56

Pollard, J, 1995b The Durrington 68 timber circle: a forgotten Late Neolithic monument, *Wiltshire Archaeol Nat Hist Mag*, **88**, 122–5

Pollard, J and Ruggles, C, 2001 Shifting perceptions: spatial order, cosmology, and patterns of deposition at Stonehenge, *Cambridge Archaeol J*, **11**, 69–90

Price, T D, Knipper, C, Grupe, G and Smrcka, V, 2004 Strontium isotopes and prehistoric human migration: the Bell Beaker period in central Europe, *European J Archaeol*, **7**, 9–40

Pryor, F, 2003 *Britain BC: life in Britain and Ireland before the Romans*. London: Harper Collins

Renfrew, C, 1968 Wessex without Mycenae, *Annals Brit Sch Athens*, **63**, 277–85

Renfrew, C, 1973 Monuments, mobilization and social organization in Neolithic Wessex, in C Renfrew (ed) *The Explanation of Culture Change: models in prehistory*. London: Duckworth, 539–58

Renfrew, C, 1976 Megaliths, territories and populations, in S J de Laet (ed) *Acculturation and Continuity in Atlantic Europe*. Bruges: De Tempel, 198–220

Reynolds, P J, 1977 Experimental archaeology and the Butser Ancient Farm Project, in J R Collis (ed) *The Iron Age in Britain: a review*. Sheffield: Sheffield Academic Press, 33–40

Richards, C, 1991 Skara Brae: revisiting a Neolithic village in Orkney, in W S Hanson and E A Slater (eds) *Scottish Archaeology: new perspectives*. Aberdeen: Aberdeen University Press, 24–47

Richards, C (ed), 2005 *Dwelling Among the Monuments: the Neolithic village of Barnhouse, Maeshowe passage grave and surrounding monuments at Stenness, Orkney*. Cambridge: McDonald Institute for Archaeological Research

Richards, C, 2010 The Ness of Brodgar – a Neolithic tribal meeting place? Kirkwall: Orkneyjar (Orkney Archaeology News) http://www.orkneyjar.com/archaeology/crnessofbrodgar.htm

Richards, C (ed) 2013 *Building the Great Stone Circles of the North*. Oxford: Windgather

Richards, C and Thomas, J S, 1984 Ritual activity and structured deposition in later Neolithic Wessex, in R Bradley and J Gardiner (eds) *Neolithic Studies: a review of some current research*. BAR Brit Ser **133**. Oxford: British Archaeological Reports, 189–218

Richards, J, 1990 *The Stonehenge Environs Project*. London: English Heritage

Richards, J, 2007 *Stonehenge: the story so far*. London: English Heritage

Richards, M P, Schulting, R J and Hedges, R E M, 2003 Sharp shift in diet at onset of Neolithic, *Nature*, **425**, 366

Ritchie, J N G, 1974 Excavation of the stone circle and cairn at Balbirnie, Fife, *Archaeol J*, **131**, 1–32

Ritchie, J N G, 1976 The Stones of Stenness, *Proc Soc Antiq Scotl*, **107**, 1–60

Roberts, C and Cox, M, 2003 *Health and Disease in Britain: from prehistory to the present day*. Stroud: Sutton

Roe, F E S, 1968 Stone mace-heads and the latest Neolithic cultures of the British Isles, in J M Coles and D D A Simpson (eds) *Studies in Ancient Europe: essays presented to Stuart Piggott*. Leicester: Leicester University Press, 145–72

Roe, F E S, 1979 Typology of stone implements with shaftholes, in Clough and Cummins (eds), 23–48

Ross, A, 1999 *Druids*. Stroud: Tempus

Ruggles, C, 1997 Astronomy and Stonehenge, in Cunliffe and Renfrew (eds), 203–29

Ruiz González, B (ed), 2009 *Dólmenes de Antequera: tutela y valorización hoy*. Sevilla: Consejería de Cultura

Scarre, C, 2011a *Landscapes of Neolithic Brittany*. Oxford: Oxford University Press

Scarre, C, 2011b The living stones of Brittany, *British Archaeology*, **121**, 36–41

Schmidt, K, 2005 'Ritual centers' and the Neolithicisation of Upper Mesopotamia, *Neo-Lithics*, **2**, 13–21

Schmidt, K, 2010 Göbekli Tepe – the Stone Age sanctuaries: new results of on-going excavations with a special focus on sculptures and high reliefs, *Documenta Praehistorica*, **37**, 239–56

Schulting, R and Wysocki, M, 2005 'In this chambered tumulus were found cleft skulls...': an assessment of the evidence for cranial trauma in the British Neolithic, *Proc Prehist Soc*, **71**, 107–38

Sharples, N M, 1991 *Maiden Castle: excavations and field survey 1985–6*. London: English Heritage

Sheridan, A, 2003 French connections I: spreading the marmites thinly, in I Armit, E Murphy, E Nelis and D D A Simpson (eds) *Neolithic Settlement in Ireland and Western Britain*. Oxford: Oxbow, 3–17

Sheridan, A, 2004 Neolithic connections along and across the Irish Sea, in V Cummings and C Fowler (eds) *The Neolithic of the Irish Sea: materiality and traditions of practice*. Oxford: Oxbow, 9–21

Sheridan, A, 2010 The Neolithization of Britain and Ireland: the 'big picture', in B Finlayson and G Warren (eds) *Landscapes in Transition*. Oxford: Oxbow, 89–105

Sherratt, A, 1990 The genesis of megaliths: monumentality, ethnicity and social complexity in Neolithic north-west Europe, *World Archaeology*, **22**, 147–67

Smith, G, 1973 Excavation of the Stonehenge avenue at West Amesbury, Wiltshire, *Wiltshire Archaeol Natur Hist Mag*, **68**, 42–56

Smith, I F and Simpson, D D A, 1966 Excavation of a round barrow on Overton Hill, north Wiltshire, *Proc Prehist Soc*, **32**, 122–55

Smith, M and Brickley, M, 2009 *People of the Long Barrows: life, death and burial in the earlier Neolithic*. Stroud: History Press

Šoberl, L, Pollard, J and Evershed, R, 2009 Pots for the afterlife: organic residue analysis of British Bronze Age pottery from funerary contexts, *Past*, **63**, 6–8

Speed, G, 2010 A Late Neolithic circular structure discovered in Rothley, Leicestershire. University of Leicester Archaeological Services http://www.le.ac.uk/ulas/projects/rothleytemplegrange.html

Stone, J F S, 1935 Some discoveries at Ratfyn, Amesbury and their bearing on the date of Woodhenge. *Wiltshire Archaeol Natur Hist Mag*, **47**, 55–67

Stone, J F S, 1938 An Early Bronze Age grave in Fargo Plantation, near Stonehenge. *Wiltshire Archaeol Natur Hist Mag*, **48**, 357–70

Stone, J F S, 1947 The Stonehenge Cursus and its affinities, *Archaeol J*, **104**, 7–19

Stone, J F S, 1949 Some Grooved Ware pottery from the Woodhenge area, *Proc Prehist Soc*, **15**, 122–7

Stone, J F S, and Young, W E V, 1948 Two pits of Grooved Ware date near Woodhenge, *Wiltshire Archaeol Natur Hist Mag*, **52**, 287–306

Stone, J F S, Piggott, S and Booth, A St J, 1954 Durrington Walls, Wiltshire: recent excavations at a ceremonial site of the early second millennium BC, *Antiq J*, **34**, 155–77

Stout, G, 2002 *Newgrange and the Bend in the Boyne*. Cork: Cork University Press

Stukeley, W, 1740 *Stonehenge: a temple restor'd to the British druids*. London: Innys & Manby

Thames Valley Archaeological Services (TVAS), 2013 Kendrew quadrangle: the henge beneath the bodies. http://www.tvas.co.uk/news/oxford-2.html

Thom, A, 1967 *Megalithic Sites in Britain*. Oxford: Oxford University Press

Thom, A, 1971 *Megalithic Lunar Observatories*. Oxford: Oxford University Press

Thom, A and Thom, A S, 1974 Stonehenge, *J Hist Astronomy*, **5**, 71–90

Thom, A and Thom, A S, 1978 *Megalithic Remains in Britain and Brittany*. Oxford: Oxford University Press

Thom, A and Thom, A S, 1988 The metrology and geometry of megalithic man, in C Ruggles (ed) *Records in Stone: papers in memory of Alexander Thom*. Cambridge: Cambridge University Press, 132–51

Thomas, H H, 1923 The source of the stones of Stonehenge, *Antiq J*, **3**, 239–60

Thomas, J S, 1999 *Understanding the Neolithic*. London: Routledge

Thomas, J S, 2003 Thoughts on the 'repacked' Neolithic revolution, *Antiquity*, **77**, 67–74

Thomas, J S, 2007 The internal features at Durrington Walls: investigations in the Southern Circle and Western Enclosures 2005–2006, in Larsson and Parker Pearson (eds), 145–57

Thomas, J S, 2010 The return of the Rinyo-Clacton folk? The cultural significance of the Grooved Ware complex in later Neolithic Britain, *Cambridge Archaeol J*, **20**, 1–15

Thomas, J S, 2013 *The Birth of Neolithic Britain: an interpretive account*. Oxford: Oxford University Press

Thomas, J S, Parker Pearson, M, Pollard, J, Richards, C, Tilley, C and Welham, K, 2009 The date of the Stonehenge cursus, *Antiquity*, **83**, 40–53

Thorpe, R S, Williams-Thorpe, O, Jenkins, D G and Watson, J S, 1991 The geological sources and transport of the bluestones of Stonehenge, Wiltshire, UK, *Proc Prehist Soc*, **57**, 103–57

Thurnam, J T, 1863 On the principal forms of ancient British and Gaulish skulls, *Memoirs Anthropol Soc London*, **1**, 120–68

Thurnam, J T, 1869 On ancient British barrows, especially those of Wiltshire and the adjoining counties (part I – long barrows), *Archaeologia*, **42**, 161–244

Tilley, C, 1994 *A Phenomenology of Landscape: places, paths and monuments*. London: Berg

Towers, J, Montgomery, J, Evans, J A, Jay, M and Parker Pearson, M, 2010 An investigation of the origins of cattle and aurochs deposited in the Early Bronze Age barrows at Gayhurst and Irthlingborough, *J Archaeol Sci*, **37**, 508–15

Towrie, S, 2008 Brodgar excavation ends, but the secrets of the ring becoming clearer. Kirkwall: Orkneyjar (Orkney Archaeology News) http://www.orkneyjar.com/archaeology/brodgar2008.htm

Towrie, S, 2010 The Ness of Brodgar – excavation background. Kirkwall: Orkneyjar (Orkney Archaeology News) http://www.orkneyjar.com/archaeology/nessofbrodgar/background.htm

Van Tilburg, J A, 1994 *Easter Island: archaeology, ecology and culture*. London & Washington DC: British Museum Press and Smithsonian Institution

Vander Linden, M, 2006 *Le Phénomène Campaniforme dans l'Europe du 3ème millénaire avant notre ère*. BAR Internat Ser **1470**. Oxford: British Archaeological Reports

Vander Linden, M, 2007 What linked the Bell Beakers in third millennium BC Europe?, *Antiquity*, **81**, 343–52

Vander Linden, M, 2012 The importance of being insular: Britain and Ireland in their north-western European context during the 3rd millennium BC, in Allen, Gardiner and Sheridan (eds), 71–84

Vatcher, F de M and Vatcher, H L, 1973 Excavation of three post-holes in Stonehenge carpark, *Wiltshire Archaeol Natur Hist Mag*, **68,** 57–63

Viner, S, Evans, J, Albarella, U and Parker Pearson, M, 2010 Cattle mobility in prehistoric Britain: strontium isotope analysis of cattle teeth from Durrington Walls (Wiltshire, Britain), *J Archaeol Sci*, **37**, 2812–20

Wainwright, G J, 1979 *Mount Pleasant, Dorset: excavations 1970–1971*. London: Society of Antiquaries

Wainwright, G J, with Longworth, I, 1971 *Durrington Walls: excavations 1966–1968*. London: Society of Antiquaries

Wainwright, G J, Evans, J G and Longworth, I H, 1971 The excavation of a Late Neolithic enclosure at Marden, Wiltshire, *Antiq J*, **51**, 177–239

West, S E, 1990 *West Stow: the prehistoric and Romano-British occupation*. East Anglian Archaeol Monogr **48**. Bury St Edmunds: East Anglian Archaeology

Whittle, A W R, 1997a Remembered and imagined belongings: Stonehenge in its traditions and structures of meaning, in Cunliffe and Renfrew (eds), 145–66

Whittle, A W R, 1997b *Sacred Mound, Holy Rings. Silbury Hill and the West Kennet palisade enclosures: a later Neolithic complex in north Wiltshire*. Oxford: Oxbow

Whittle, A W R and Cummings, V (eds), 2007 *Going Over: the Mesolithic–Neolithic transition in north-west Europe*. Oxford: British Academy & Oxford University Press

Whittle, A W R, Atkinson, R J C, Chambers, R and Thomas, N, 1992 Excavations in the Neolithic and Bronze Age complex at Dorchester-on-Thames, Oxfordshire, 1947–1952 and 1981, *Proc Prehist Soc*, **58**, 143–201

Whittle, A W R, Barclay, A, Bayliss, A, McFadyen, L, Schulting, R and Wysocki, M, 2007 Building for the dead: events, processes and changing worldviews from the thirty-eighth to the thirty-fourth centuries cal. BC in southern Britain, *Cambridge Archaeol J*, **17** (Suppl), 123–47

Whittle, A W R, Healy, F and Bayliss, A, 2011 *Gathering Time: dating the early Neolithic enclosures of southern Britain and Ireland*. Oxford, Oxbow

Whittle, A W R, Pollard, J and Grigson, C, 1999 *The Harmony of Symbols: the Windmill Hill causewayed enclosure*. Oxford: Oxbow

Williams-Thorpe, O, Jones, M C, Potts, P J and Webb, P C, 2006 Preseli dolerite bluestones: axe-heads, Stonehenge monoliths, and outcrop sources, *Oxford J Archaeol*, **25**, 29–46

Woodward, A B and Woodward, P J, 1996 The topography of some barrow cemeteries in Bronze Age Wessex, *Proc Prehist Soc*, **62**, 275–92

Woodward, P J, Davies, S M and Graham, A H, 1993 *Excavations at the Old Methodist Chapel and Greyhound Yard, Dorchester, 1981–1984*. Dorchester: Dorset Archaeology and Natural History Society

Wright, N, 2007 *Geoffrey Of Monmouth, The History of the Kings of Britain* (ed Michael D Reeve). An edition and translation of *De gestis Britonum [Historia regum Britanniae]*, Arthurian Studies **69**. Woodbridge: Boydell and Brewer

Yates, D T, 2007 *Land, Power and Prestige: Bronze Age field systems in southern England*. Oxford: Oxbow

Young, W E V, 1935 The Stonehenge car park excavation, 1935, *in* Leaves from My Journal VII. Manuscript diary, Library of the Wiltshire Archaeological and Natural History Society (Devizes)